Constructing
Bathrooms

WILLIAM P. SPENCE

Sterling Publishing Co., Inc.
New York

DISCLAIMER

Although the information presented in the following pages was provided by a wide range of reliable sources, including material and tool manufacturers, professional and trade associations, and government agencies, it should be noted that the use of tools and materials in home-maintenance activities involves some risk of injury. The reader should also always observe the local building codes, the operating instructions of equipment manufacturers, and directions of the companies supplying the materials. The author and publisher assume no liability for the accuracy of the material included.

Library of Congress Cataloging-in-Publication Data

Spence, William Perkins, 1925–
    Constructing bathrooms / William P. Spence.
        p. cm. — (Building basics)
    Includes index.
    ISBN 0-8069-8103-2
    1. Bathrooms—Design and construction. 2. Bathrooms—Remodeling.
    I. Title. II Series.
TH4816.3.B37 S64 2001
643'.52—dc21   00-048260

Designed by Judy Morgan
Edited by Rodman Neumann

1 3 5 7 9 10 8 6 4 2

Published by Sterling Publishing Company, Inc.
387 Park Avenue South, New York, N.Y. 10016
© 2001 by William P. Spence
Distributed in Canada by Sterling Publishing
c/o Canadian Manda Group, One Atlantic Avenue, Suite 105
Toronto, Ontario, Canada M6K 3E7
Distributed in Great Britain and Europe by Cassell PLC
Wellington House, 125 Strand, London WC2R 0BB, England
Distributed in Australia by Capricorn Link (Australia) Pty Ltd.
P.O. Box 6651, Baulkham Hills, Business Centre, NSW 2153, Australia
Printed in China
All rights reserved

Sterling ISBN 0-8069-8103-2

Contents

CHAPTER 1

Preliminary Considerations

Courtesy American Standard, Inc.

When planning a new house you have considerable freedom to select the shape and size of the area to form a bathroom. You have the opportunity to do more than limit yourself to the traditional rectangle (1-1). If you are remodeling, you usually have to rearrange fixtures and cabinets within the original space unless you can move a wall that enlarges the area or add a small addition to the house. In all cases observe the principles of good planning and make a study of the many fixtures and cabinets available. The choice is wide and varied. Basically you have to decide what you want in a bath. One bath may be a small room for guests and occasional use during the day (1-2). Another may be your pride and

1-1 A bathroom can be a spacious, interesting room that is warm and inviting. The use of quality fixtures, natural woods, carefully selected colors, and natural light all contribute to the restful atmosphere.

joy and be off the master bedroom. It can have a whirlpool, dual lavatories, the toilet in a private compartment, and luxurious lighting (**1-3**).

Remember you must meet local building codes such as electrical and plumbing requirements. Ventilation is another important item. While windows in bathrooms are highly recommended you still need some form of mechanical ventilation. Mechanical ventilation in bathrooms with no windows is mandatory.

Courtesy Kohler Company

1-2 These fixtures fit nicely into a small powder room for guests and occasional use by the family. The pedestal lavatory requires a minimum of space, which helps when planning the layout.

Courtesy Jacuzzi Whirlpool Bath

1-3 This bathroom features a large whirlpool bath, a pedestal lavatory, and a toilet set in a compartment. Natural lighting enhances the area.

Fixtures and cabinets are manufactured in a wide range of styles and sizes and from a number of different materials. Part of the initial planning is to make some choices of brands, sizes, and materials. These choices will influence somewhat the overall layout of the bathroom. Remember, you can get custom-built cabinets for uses as having two lavatories or special storage facilities (1-4).

If you are planning a new bathroom, begin by listing the features you want and deciding which fixtures and cabinets are needed to meet your requirements. If you are remodeling, you certainly know what you do not like about the existing bathroom. Write these things down. Then set in writing how you want to improve the bathroom by the new layout and new fixtures and cabinets. One frequent problem with older bathrooms is the location of the door. Moving it is relatively easy and can make a great improvement in the layout.

In both cases visit several local plumbing fixture and cabinet retail outlets and pick up the dozens of color brochures they have available. From these you will get some very good ideas, not only placement and fixture choice, but the use of color and lighting.

1-4 These cherry cabinets provide considerable storage for items needed in the bathroom. Notice the cherry-wood boxing around the tub.

Eventually you will end up with layout and fixture and cabinet choices. Get the prices because some are very expensive. Work out the total cost. If it is a new house this will become part of the builder's contract. If it is a remodel job you will most likely buy these. Then get estimates from several licensed electricians and plumbers. A final cost on a remodeling project will include what you do with the walls and floor. As discussed, find out your options, make choices, and get firm costs.

SHAPE OF THE ROOM

Consider the shape of the room. Rectangular shapes are most frequently used and are quite satisfactory for the average small or medium-size bathroom. However, if you want something a bit better do not feel restrained from using other shapes. As you study the design principles keep in mind that some variation in the shape of the room can be used to improve the layout and appearance (1-5).

Courtesy Merillat Industries

1-5 The designer used a series of curved cabinets and an irregular room shape to produce this interesting bathroom.

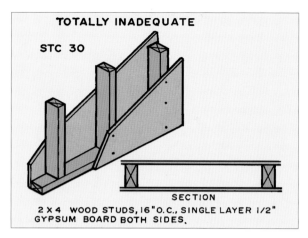

TOTALLY INADEQUATE

STC 30

SECTION

2 X 4 WOOD STUDS, 16"O.C., SINGLE LAYER 1/2" GYPSUM BOARD BOTH SIDES.

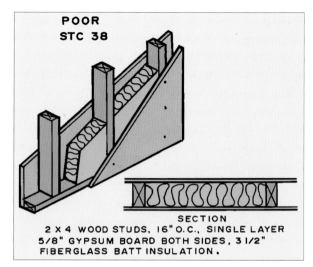

POOR
STC 38

SECTION

2 X 4 WOOD STUDS, 16"O.C., SINGLE LAYER 5/8" GYPSUM BOARD BOTH SIDES, 3 1/2" FIBERGLASS BATT INSULATION.

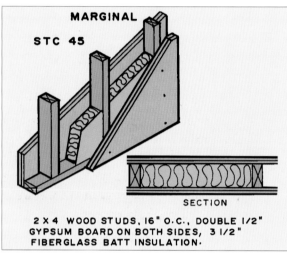

MARGINAL

STC 45

SECTION

2 X 4 WOOD STUDS, 16" O.C., DOUBLE 1/2" GYPSUM BOARD ON BOTH SIDES, 3 1/2" FIBERGLASS BATT INSULATION.

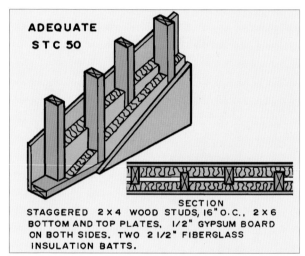

ADEQUATE
STC 50

SECTION

STAGGERED 2 X 4 WOOD STUDS, 16"O.C., 2 X 6 BOTTOM AND TOP PLATES, 1/2" GYPSUM BOARD ON BOTH SIDES. TWO 2 1/2" FIBERGLASS INSULATION BATTS.

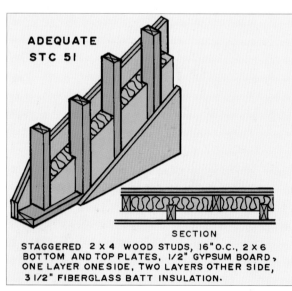

ADEQUATE
STC 51

SECTION

STAGGERED 2 X 4 WOOD STUDS, 16"O.C., 2 X 6 BOTTOM AND TOP PLATES, 1/2" GYPSUM BOARD, ONE LAYER ONE SIDE, TWO LAYERS OTHER SIDE, 3 1/2" FIBERGLASS BATT INSULATION.

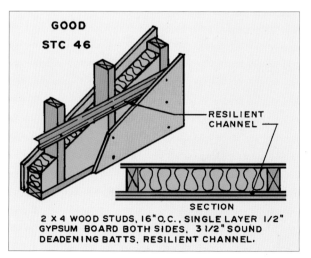

GOOD
STC 46

RESILIENT CHANNEL

SECTION

2 X 4 WOOD STUDS, 16"O.C., SINGLE LAYER 1/2" GYPSUM BOARD BOTH SIDES, 3 1/2" SOUND DEADENING BATTS, RESILIENT CHANNEL.

1-6 (Above and opposite page) Several typical wall constructions used to reduce the transmission of sound between rooms.

TABLE 1-1 SOUND TRANSMISSION CLASS (STC) & NOISE CONTROL RATINGS.

Sound Transmission Class (STC)	Speech Audibility	Noise Control Rating
15 to 25	Normal speech easily understood	Poor
25 to 35	Loud speech easily understood Normal speech 50% understood	Marginal
35 to 45	Loud speech 50% understood Normal speech faintly heard, but not understood	Good
45 to 55	Loud speech faintly heard, but not understood Normal speech usually inaudible	Very good
55 and up	Loud speech usually inaudible	Excellent

SOUND TRANSMISSION

Also remember to build walls that will reduce the transfer of sound to the rooms on all sides. Several relatively easy ways to do this are shown in **1-6**. These examples show ratings using fiberglass insulation. Sound transmission characteristics are specified in terms of the wall's Sound Transmission Class (STC). The higher the STC rating the greater the ability to limit the transmission of sound. STC ratings are specified in **Table 1-1**. Bathroom walls should have an STC ratings 52 or greater.

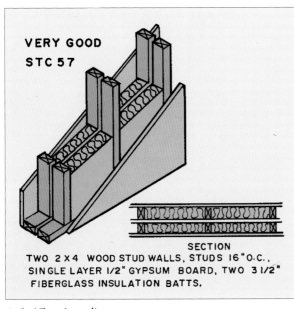

VERY GOOD STC 57

SECTION
TWO 2 X 4 WOOD STUD WALLS, STUDS 16"O.C., SINGLE LAYER 1/2" GYPSUM BOARD, TWO 3 1/2" FIBERGLASS INSULATION BATTS.

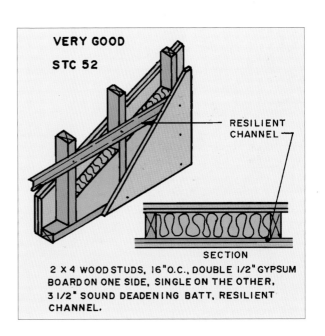

VERY GOOD STC 52

RESILIENT CHANNEL

SECTION
2 X 4 WOOD STUDS, 16"O.C., DOUBLE 1/2" GYPSUM BOARD ON ONE SIDE, SINGLE ON THE OTHER, 3 1/2" SOUND DEADENING BATT, RESILIENT CHANNEL.

1-6 (Continued)

1-7 These Noise Reducer™ sound-deadening batts will greatly reduce sound transmission through interior walls.

Courtesy Certainteed Corporation

If you use sound-reducing batts as shown in **1-7**, sound transmission through the walls will be reduced even more.

CONSIDER FLOOR LOADS

The floor needs to be reinforced to carry the weight of the bathtub or whirlpool. Some whirlpools are very large and hold many gallons of water. Water weighs 62.4 pounds per cubic foot or about 8.3 pounds per gallon. Check out the weight of a full whirlpool before you buy it.

MAKE A LIST

As you begin thinking about the bathroom make a list of things important to you and record possible decisions. Examples of what you will most likely consider are listed in **Table 1-2**.

As you review the needs and possibilities write the recommendations you reach and other related information. In some cases you may list more than one possible requirement and finalize it later. Do not forget to consider the accessories that are required for a functional bathroom.

TYPICAL TYPES OF BATHROOM

A house will usually contain at least two of the following types of bathroom:

1. Master bedroom bath suite
2. General family bathroom serving several bedrooms
3. A powder room
4. The universally accessible bathroom

The **master bedroom bath suite** is designed to fit into the overall plan for the master bedroom and any special storage such as walk-in closets, dressing rooms, and storage cabinets. In a new house it is planned as a part of the overall design and related to the exterior, the master bedroom, and the overall floor plan. In a remodeling job

TABLE 1-2 THINGS TO CONSIDER ABOUT THE BATHROOM: MAKE A LIST

1. Who will use it?
    Is it for the master bedroom?
    Will it be serving several bedrooms?
    Will guests use it during periods of entertainment (powder room)?

2. Consider the physical limitations of family members.
    For example, a large shower with easy access and a seat may be needed.

3. What fixtures other than the toilet, lavatory, and tub or shower are needed?
    Consider a whirlpool or a luxury shower (refer to **2-1**).

4. Consider any styling ideas you may have found in magazines or books.
    Also list color and decoration features.

5. What do you plan to store in the bathroom?

6. Consider what type and style of cabinets you want.

7. What style of fixtures do you prefer?

8. Consider the size of the room.
    How much clear floor area do you want to allow?
    Beyond the minimums in the planning guidelines?

9. What design features do you want?
    Do you want the toilet in a private compartment?
    Consider if you want a large custom-built tile shower?

10. What type of wall finish and floor finish is desired?

11. Is there any limit on cost?
    On particular fixtures?
    The overall job cost?

12. The shape of the room.
    Do you want the typical rectangluar-shaped bathroom?
    Would you find a different shape more interesting?

13. Do you want to allow for natural light?
    Through windows or a skylight?

14. What type and style of accessories are required or desired?

15. If it is a remodel job, do you want to use the existing room?
    Or do you want to move some walls or add additional space?

16. What type and style of lighting do you prefer?
    Do you want general illumination, special lighting at mirrors, decorative lighting?

the suite is often added to the master bedroom as an addition to the house. It can involve moving walls or absorbing a large closet or even adding a small room next to the master bedroom.

The master bedroom bath suite is usually large, has multiple fixtures, and is rather extravagant. It exists for the comfort and pleasure of the occupant (**1-8**).

The **general family bathroom** tends to have fixtures spaced so that it may under certain circumstances be used by two people. For example, the tub or shower and toilet could be locat-

1-8 A bathroom to serve the master bedroom should be spacious and have high-quality fixtures. Notice these fixtures have a light-blue tint that is echoed by the darker-blue walls.

ed in one space and one or more lavatories be in a separate space within the room (1-9). This provides two private compartments allowing two people to use the bath at the same time. Some place the toilet by itself in a private compartment.

Family bathrooms require you to give consideration to the needs of children. A small platform in front of one lavatory will help and can be removed as the children grow up. A shower instead of a tub or in addition to a tub will help them. Fixtures that can be adjusted for height are available.

Courtesy Kohler Company

1-9 This family bathroom has two pedestal lavatories separated by a cabinet enabling two people to use the bathroom at the same time.

One helpful idea to reduce congestion in the family bathroom is to locate a small lavatory and mirror in each bedroom.

Rather than one large family bathroom, some prefer to build two smaller rooms each complete but using minimum spacing requirements (1-10).

A **powder room** is also referred to as a **half-bath**. It will have a lavatory and toilet and be allowed only minimum clear floor area, although some extra space is recommended. It is typically located near the area where you entertain, and so falls near the living room, family room, or other large-size room. The entrance should somehow be screened or off a hall so when guests use it they can do so with some degree of privacy. When used for the family to supplement the other bathrooms rather than for guests, it can be placed in a utility room, under a stair, or in some other less valuable but still accessible space. Some like to make it accessible from outside so children playing in the yard can access it without running through the house.

1-10 This bathroom has the required three fixtures carefully arranged so as to not require a large floor area. The black fixtures and the white walls and floor provide an interesting room.

CONSTRUCTING BATHROOMS

The **universally accessible bathroom** is designed for use by almost anyone regardless of physical condition. It meets all the requirements of the U.S. Disabilities Act. It will accommodate children because the height of fixtures is varied and large enough for wheelchair users to maneuver. A typical example of a universally accessible bathroom is in **1-11**.

1-11 This bathroom has a shower with a seat and grab bars and a tub with a seat and grab bars making it accessible to those with physical limitations. Considerable floor area is needed for wheelchair users.

CHAPTER 2

Planning Guidelines

Once you have a good idea of what you want (2-1), you can make drawings of a potential layout. This is the time to consider recommended spacing and other guidelines that can help you develop a workable layout that is efficient and comfortable. Guidelines to assist planners in this process have been developed by The National Kitchen and Bath Association.

Courtesy Alumax Bath Enclosures

NATIONAL KITCHEN & BATH ASSOCIATION

Many of the design recommendations in this chapter and in parts of other chapters were developed from those in National Kitchen and Bath Association (NKBA) publications, with their permission. The National Kitchen and Bath Association is a professional organization representing over 7,000 industry professionals across the United States and Canada, including manufacturers and their products, dealers, and designers. For more on the NKBA, see the section on additional information, on page 139.

2-1 Plan for luxury items you may want, such as a custom shower or a whirlpool.

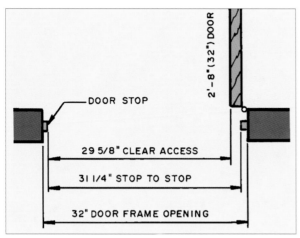

2-2 A typical 2'-8" door will not give a clear 32-inch opening as is recommended for access by wheelchair users.

DOOR OPENING REQUIREMENTS

As the following recommendations will show, a 32-inch-wide door is minimum. For successful use by wheelchair users this should be clear of the door stop and the edge of the door in an open position. Notice in **2-2** that a 32-inch-wide door and frame actually only give a clear opening of 29⅝ inches. A 36-inch-wide door is the best choice to make the bath wheelchair accessible. A typical wheelchair with a person's hands on the wheels is 30 inches wide.

Pocket doors may be helpful when trying to get the full 32-inch width. However, they are more difficult to use than swinging doors.

Since it is not always possible to allow the ideal clear floor space at the door, more limited recommendations are shown in **2-3** and **2-4**.

In **2-3** notice the clear space at the door should not have a cabinet or fixture wider than 24 inches alongside the direction of travel. If the cabinet or fixture along the wall in the direction of travel is longer than 24 inches, the entrance aisle should be 36 in. wide or wider (**2-4**). These are not ideal and will make it difficult for some people to maneuver within the area allowed.

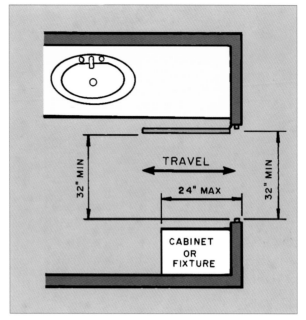

2-3 This access is not ideal and will cause limited access problems for some people.

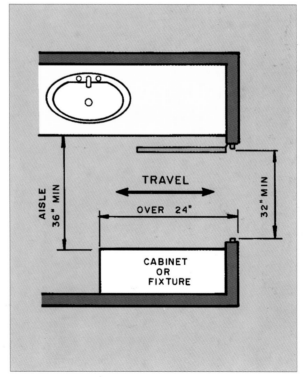

2-4 If a cabinet along the flow of traffic is longer than 24" be certain to have an aisle at least 36 inches wide.

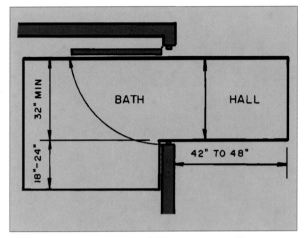

2-5 A bath entrance should have an open floor area the width of the door and a wider area on the latch side.

Ideally the floor of the bath should have a clear space the width of the door opening and 48 to 60 inches long. A second clear space on the latch side of the door should be 18 to 24 inches wide as shown in **2-5**.

LAVATORY CLEARANCES

The minimum clear floor space in front of a lavatory is shown in **2-6**. This can run parallel with or perpendicular to the fixture. When you have two lavatories in a single cabinet you will want to allow at least 60 inches of clear floor space parallel to the cabinet with the lavatories 30 inches apart (**2-7**). Typically this distance is made larger for a more private and luxurious installation. A lavatory should be at least 15 inches from a side wall as shown in **2-7**.

Lavatories for wheelchair users require at least 8 inches of knee space below the lavatory sink. This may be accomplished by using a wall-hung unit or a base cabinet with a lavatory installed in the top (**2-8**). The minimum floor space at a lavatory can include some of the open area below the lavatory as part of the recommended minimum open floor area (**2-9**).

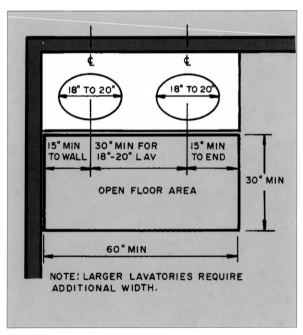

2-6 A 30 × 48 inch open floor area is recommended in front of a lavatory.

2-7 When you have two lavatories side by side you need at least 60 inches of open floor area to comfortably use both at the same time.

CONSTRUCTING BATHROOMS

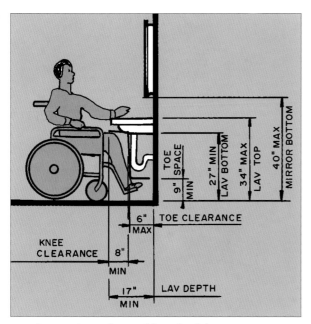

2-8 Lavatories to be used by wheelchair users require toe and knee space and protection for the legs.

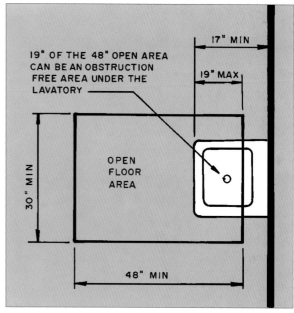

2-9 Some of the obstruction-free floor area under a lavatory can be considered part of the overall recommended open floor area.

LAVATORY COUNTER & MIRROR HEIGHTS

The height of the lavatory cabinet can be varied to suit the needs of the user. For some a 30-inch height is comfortable and for others up to 40 in. is best. Usually family members vary in height so some make one lower than the other (2-10). A height of 32 inches is commonly used, as seen in 2-11, on the following page. Pedestal lavatories are typically 32 to 36 inches high (2-12).

2-10 You may want to have multiple lavatories on different heights to make them easier to use.

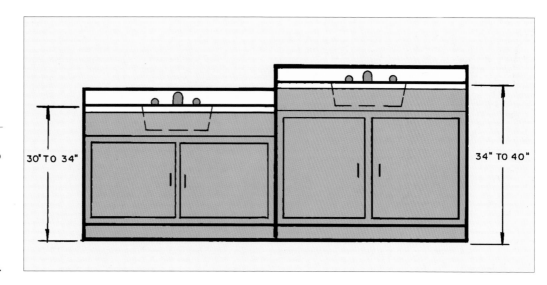

2-11 This is a standard 32-inch-high lavatory cabinet.

2-12 Pedestal lavatories are available in several heights. They provide open floor area on all sides.

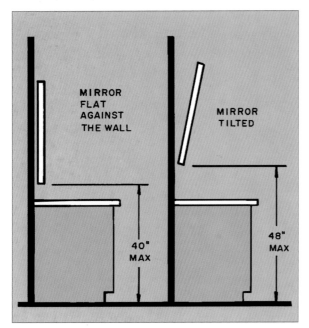

2-13 If you tilt the mirror, you can place it higher on the wall. Try several heights until you find the one best for you.

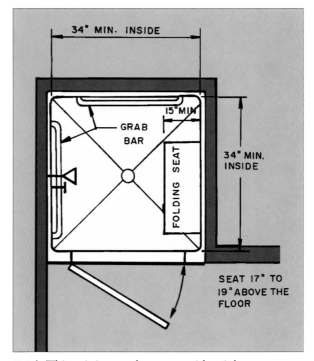

2-14 This minimum shower provides tight quarters.

The bottom edge of a mirror mounted flat against the wall should not be more than 40 inches above the floor. If you tilt it some, you can raise it up to 48 inches (**2-13**). Experiment before hanging to get the best height for the family members. Tilting the mirror also makes it usable by wheelchair users.

SHOWER RECOMMENDATIONS

The minimum dimensions needed for an enclosed shower are shown in **2-14**. The grab bars or a folding seat, if present, may project into this minimum size. Typical larger sizes (**2-15**),

2-15 Larger showers are more convenient to use and can provide easy access.

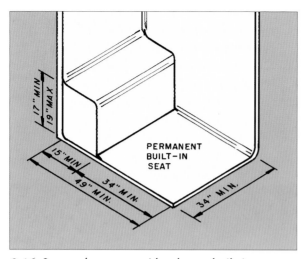

which are as much as 34 × 50 inches or 34 × 62 inches, provide much needed space for bathing and seats.

Larger showers will have a seat sized as shown in **2-16**. Permanent built-in seats should not encroach on the minimum 34 × 34 inches clear shower floor area. Shower doors should open into a clear floor space in the bathroom.

A minimum shower for wheelchair users is shown in **2-17**. Notice a 36-inch clear door is required. The person goes straight in and turns facing the controls and showerhead. A better arrangement is shown in **2-18**. This shower is

2-16 Larger showers provide a larger, built-in seat providing additional safety and comfort.

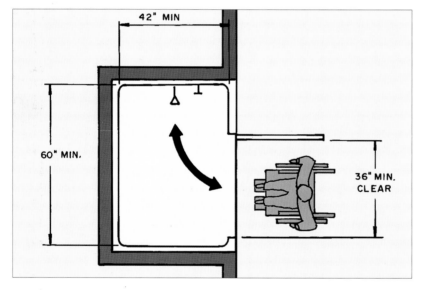

2-17 This shower provides minimum access for wheelchair users.

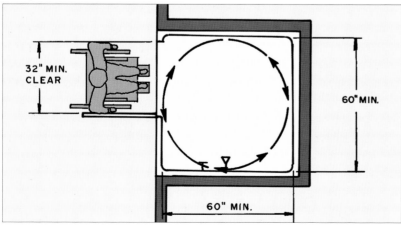

2-18 A shower 60 inches square enables a wheelchair user to maneuver inside it.

large enough to permit the wheelchair to rotate 360°. It can go straight in, rotate, shower, rotate, and leave facing forward.

Shower controls should be easy to reach from inside and outside the shower. They must be no lower than 36 inches or higher than 48 inches above the floor. The showerhead is typically 72 to 78 inches above the floor (2-19). If the shower has a built-in hand-held showerhead it is usually 48 inches above the floor. If it does not, you will have to install it at the showerhead. Grab bars are located 33 to 36 inches above the floor.

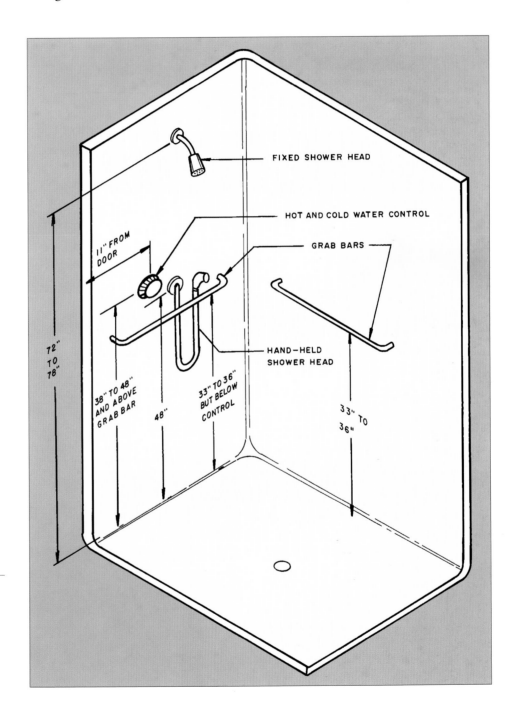

2-19 Locate the shower controls, showerhead, and grab bars as shown to provide easy-to-use controls and safety.

BATHTUB RECOMMENDATIONS

The size and shape of the clear floor space required beside a bathtub depends upon the direction from which you have to approach it.

If it is located so you walk along the side (parallel) a clear space of 30 × 60 inches is minimum (2-20). Should you have to walk perpendicular to it, the minimum floor area is as shown in 2-21. If a cabinet has a recessed area providing an unobstructed floor area, at least

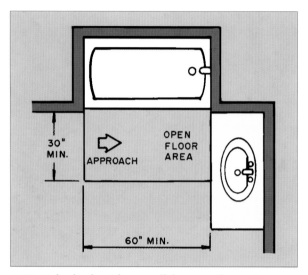

2-20 A bathtub with a parallel approach requires at least a 30 × 60 inch open floor area. Increase this area, if possible.

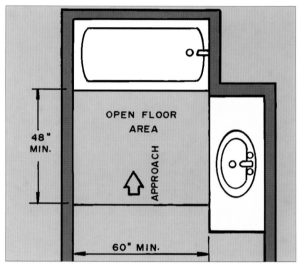

2-21 If you approach perpendicular to the bathtub, you need a minimum of 48 × 60 inches of open floor area.

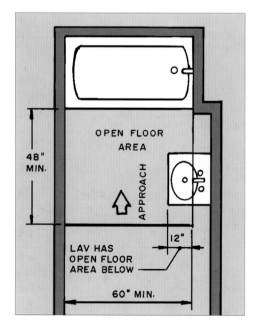

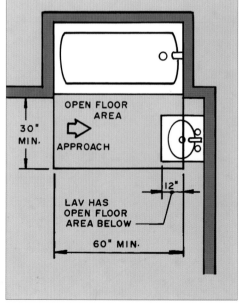

2-22 You can use 12 inches of open floor area below a cabinet by the bathtub as part of the minimum open floor area.

CONSTRUCTING BATHROOMS

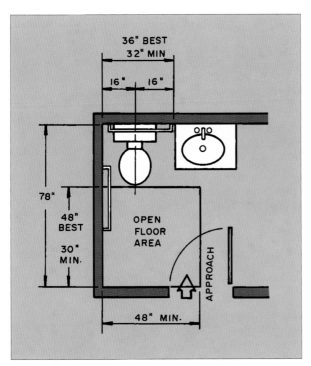

2-23 This shows the minimum open floor area in front of a toilet when you approach it from the front.

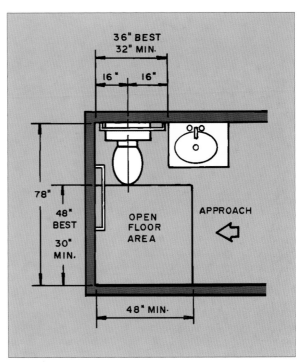

2-24 When you approach a toilet from the side you need at least a 48 × 48 inch open floor area.

12 inches of this can be counted as part of the overall minimum clear floor area (2-22). Remember, these are minimums. If you can allow larger clear floor areas the bathroom will be greatly improved.

TOILET & BIDET RECOMMENDATIONS

The minimum clear floor space in front of the toilet is 48 × 48 inches as shown in 2-23 and 2-24. If it is not possible to get the full 48 inches in front, this can be reduced some. The National Kitchen and Bath Association recommends you never go below 30 inches.

The clear floor area can have a door swing over it because the door is closed after you enter the bathroom (refer to 2-23). Up to 12 inches of the clear floor space can extend under a nearby lavatory or cabinet (2-25).

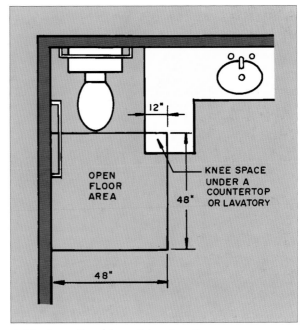

2-25 A small portion of the clear floor space at a toilet can extend under a nearby cabinet that has open floor area below it.

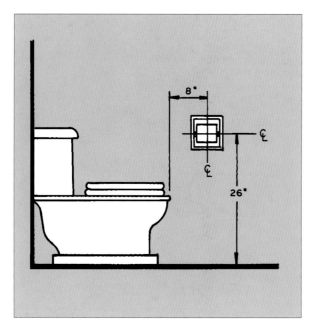

2-26 Locate the tissue holder so it is easily accessible.

A recommended location for the toilet paper holder is in **2-26**.

The principles applying to a toilet all apply to a bidet. The ideal situation is shown in **2-27** with the 30-inch clearance as an absolute minimum. The open floor area for the toilet and bidet can overlap as long as the centerline of the bidet is 16 inches from the centerline of the toilet.

A toilet should have at least a 32-inch-wide clear wall space. While 30 inches is acceptable it may not allow for full use by some people (**2-23**). A 36-inch wall space is highly recommended. If the toilet is to be built into a privacy compartment it should be a minimum of 36

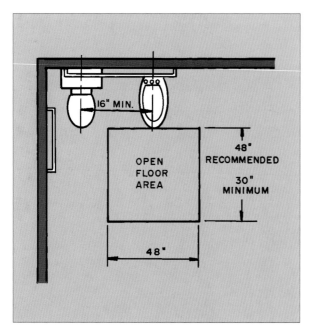

2-27 A bidet requires at least a 30 × 48 inch open floor area. A larger open floor area is recommended. This area can overlap the toilet open floor area.

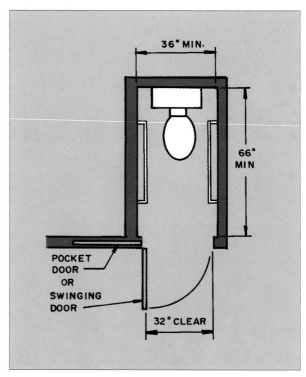

2-28 A toilet in a compartment requires at least 36 inches clear width. A wider compartment is recommended.

inches wide (**2-28**). Privacy toilet compartments should be sized to allow the occupant some room to move about. The one shown in **2-29** will serve the person who does not use a wheelchair. The one shown in **2-30** will permit a wheelchair user to enter and provide minimum space for mobility.

Generally the toilet and the bidet are placed side by side. This requires less total clear floor area and simplifies the plumbing. The recommended spacing of these fixtures is shown in **2-31**. The 32-inch minimum wall space can overlap provided the minimum clear floor area is available for each.

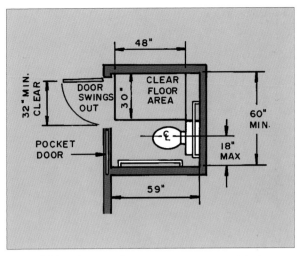

2-29 This privacy toilet compartment provides adequate room for comfortable use.

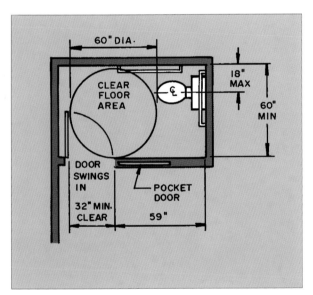

2-30 This privacy toilet compartment is accessible to wheelchair users.

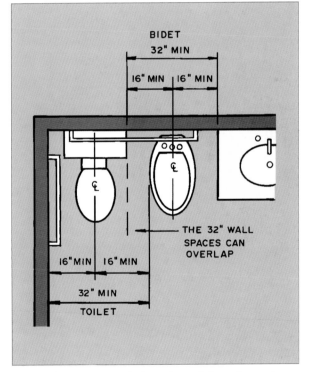

2-31 The recommended spacing of the toilet and bidet when they are placed side by side is 32 inches. However, 16 inches of this can overlap.

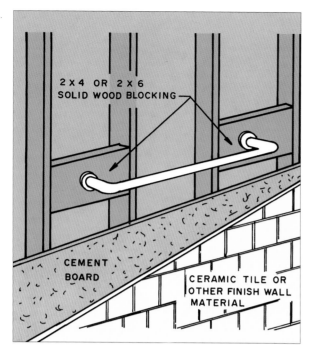

LOCATING & INSTALLING GRAB BARS

Grab bars are essential in bathrooms where people need support and protection from falling. The *U.S. American Disabilities Act Guidelines for Buildings and Facilities* sets forth detailed requirements for locating grab bars.

First the walls must have 2-inch-thick solid-wood blocking secured between the wall studs at the location of each grab bar or have the wall covered with ¾-inch-thick plywood (**2-32**). The grab bar should be able to support at least 300 lbs. Gypsum wallboard or cement tile backer boards are not acceptable bases for support. A grab bar should be 1¼ or 1½ inches in diameter and have 1½ inches of space between the bar and the wall (**2-33**).

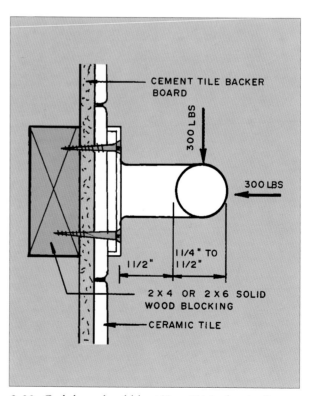

2-32 (Top and bottom) Grab bars are securely screwed to ¾-inch plywood panels or solid-wood blocking.

2-33 Grab bars should be 1¼ to 1½ inches in diameter and provide 1½ inches of space at the wall.

An example of grab bars at at a toilet and their placement generally for toilets are shown in **2-34** and **2-35**. On the following pages there are examples and the recommended placement for showers shown in **2-36** and **2-37**, and for bathtubs in **2-38** and **2-39**.

Refer also to Chapter 3 for more photos showing various accessories that are available to help improve the safe use of bathroom facilities.

Courtesy HEWI, Inc.

2-34 Grab bars can extend beside the toilet if there is no adjacent wall.

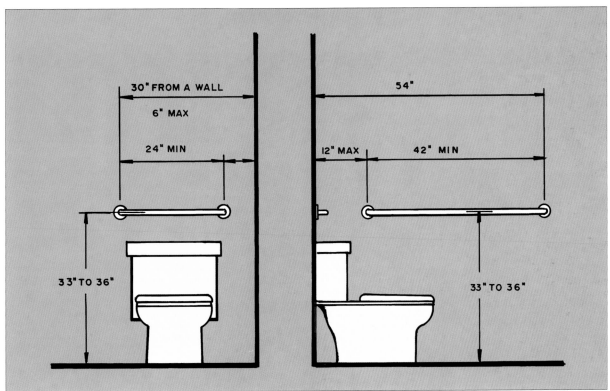

30" FROM A WALL

6" MAX

24" MIN

33" TO 36"

54"

12" MAX   42" MIN

33" TO 36"

2-35 Recommended placement of grab bars around the toilet.

Courtesy HEWI, Inc.

Courtesy HEWI, Inc.

2-36 Both of these examples of colored grab bars and seats in the shower are made of nylon.

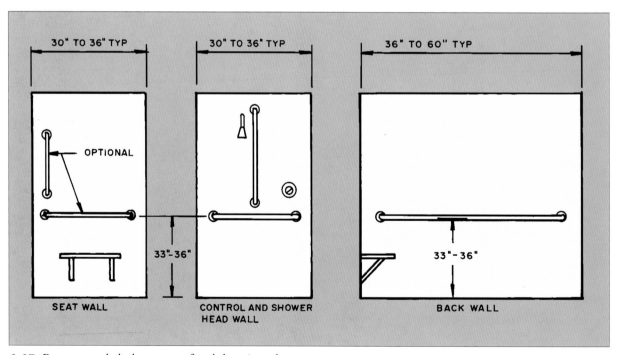

30" TO 36" TYP

30" TO 36" TYP

36" TO 60" TYP

OPTIONAL

33"–36"

33"–36"

SEAT WALL

CONTROL AND SHOWER
HEAD WALL

BACK WALL

2-37 Recommended placement of grab bars in a shower.

2-38 Garb bars around the bathtub allow access with a minimum of difficulty.

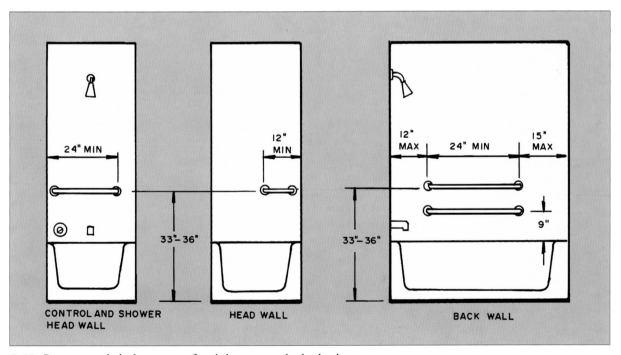

2-39 Recommended placement of grab bars around a bathtub.

Courtesy Wellborn Cabinet, Inc.

2-40 The lavatory base has a storage drawer and additional storage is provided by the base and wall cabinets on each side. The vanity has some storage and a tall cabinet beside it. These cabinets are finished in a color described as harvest maple.

STORAGE IDEAS

You will need to incorporate in your plan some storage cabinets for towels, toiletries, soap, and other supplies. If the room is large, base cabinets and wall cabinets add a great deal (**2-40**). For most bathrooms, the lavatory vanity cabinets will be the major storage center, especially if the cabinet is longer than the minimum needed for the lavatory bowl (**2-41**). There are many variations of small wall-hung cabinets that are good for medicines and other small articles (**2-42**).

2-41 This small lavatory cabinet provides considerable storage.

2-42 These individual wall-hung cabinets are typical of the many such storage units available that are very useful in a bathroom.

CHAPTER 3

Cabinets, Countertops & Accessories

Cabinet manufacturers have designed and built many sizes and styles of cabinets suitable for use in a bathroom. The basic unit is the vanity that may hold one or more lavatories (3-1). You can also have custom-built cabinets.

Cabinets typically have particleboard sides, back and bottom, and solid wood frames, drawer fronts, and doors. The exposed panels may have wood laminates or high-pressure plastic laminates bonded to them.

A vanity reserved for personal grooming is a popular unit (3-1). It will have many drawers, a mirror, and special lighting.

Cabinets are produced in three ways. They may be **mass produced** in a manufacturing plant, **built on the site** by a cabinetmaker, or be **custom built** by a cabinetmaker in a local cabinet shop.

Mass-produced cabinets are manufactured using industrial woodworking machinery where each piece is precision cut and assembled in a factory Manufactured cabinets are available in three grades. The **economy grade** is the lowest and least expensive.

Courtesy Wellborn Cabinet, Inc.

3-1 Cabinetry can reduce the "bathroom" look of the room. The lavatory cabinet is surrounded by tall cabinets, providing considerable storage. Notice the matching vanity for personal grooming.

It is a good solid unit but the materials and joinery are not up to the better grades. The **custom grade** has better joinery and higher-quality framing. The **premium grade** uses the best materials and joinery techniques.

The Architectural Woodwork Institute has done much through the years to establish quality standards through research and testing. They maintain a certification program assuring the cabinets are made to the established standards.

The size of a typical bath lavatory vanity is shown in **3-2**. The vanity is often made higher for easier use by tall people. Cabinet manufacturers have available other cabinets used for storage in the bathroom as shown in **3-1**. As you plan your bathroom, visit several cabinet dealers and get brochures showing what they have available. You will find a good variety of designs and finishes. Question the quality of construction as you get prices.

FACEFRAME & FRAMELESS CABINETS

Manufactured and custom-built cabinets are available with and without a faceframe. Those with faceframes are most widely used. Framing for a cabinet with a faceframe is shown in **3-3**. In most examples of cabinets the sides and bottom will be ½-inch to ⅝-inch particleboard with a ¼-inch hardboard or plywood back. The faceframe is typically made of ¾-inch solid wood.

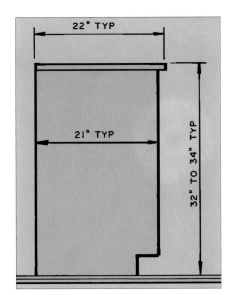

3-2 (Above) This is the commonly used size bathroom lavatory vanity. Taller units are available for taller people.

3-3 (Right) This cabinet has a solid wood faceframe secured to the edges of the bulkheads and partitions.

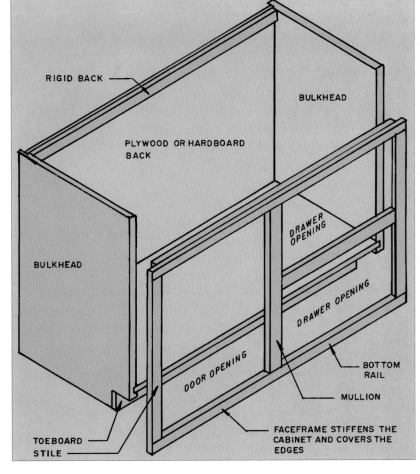

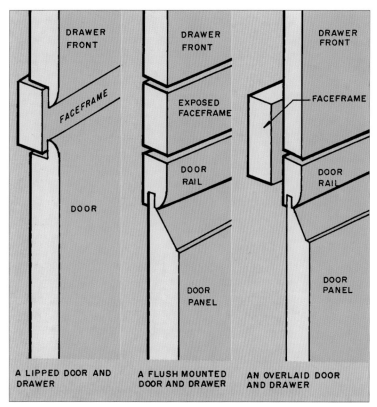

3-4 The doors and drawers used in faceframe construction can overlap or be used flush with the faceframe.

3-5 This vanity has a faceframe and lipped doors and drawers. Notice the doors are paneled and the edges of the drawers shaped.

The doors and drawers fit over the faceframe, as shown in **3-4**. The vanity in **3-5** has a faceframe and lipped doors and drawers.

The frameless cabinet does not have a faceframe. It is modeled on a European-style unit often based on a repeating 32mm unit, as described below.

32mm SYSTEM

Cabinets with a faceframe are often referred to as "traditional cabinets," whereas frameless cabinets are sometimes called "European cabinets." This is simply because frameless construction first became popular in Europe; however, since the frameless construction is based on a repeating 32mm unit, professional cabinetmakers refer to this as the 32mm system.

The 32mm system produces cabinets using flat panels and standardized measurements in increments of 32mm. The cabinet is joined by drilling dowel holes spaced 32mm apart, center to center, along the butting edges of the carcass. These are drilled with a multiple-spindle drilling machine so that all the holes in one piece are drilled at the same time. Likewise the shelves are adjustable and sit on pins in rows of dowel holes spaced 32mm on center.

This system uses precision woodworking machinery that permits fast setups and accurate machining. Specially designed hardware enables cabinets to be produced faster and at less cost than conventional methods using a faceframe.

Since the frameless cabinet does not have a faceframe, the carcass has to use ¾-inch particleboard sides and bottom. The back is typically

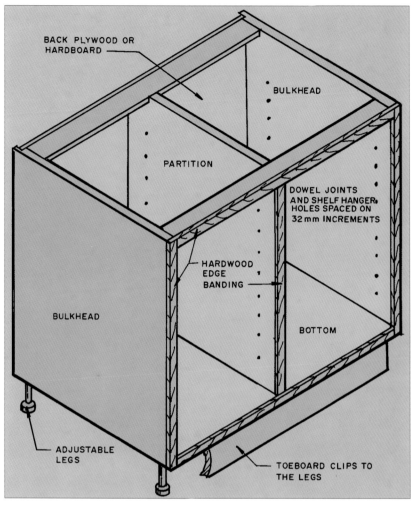

3-6 Typical framing for a frameless cabinet.

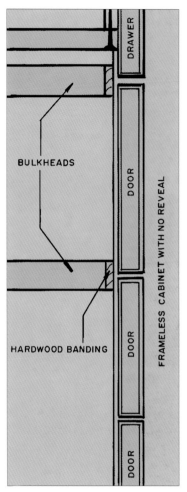

3-7 Doors and drawers used with frameless construction can be installed with no reveal.

¼- or ⅜-inch plywood, which provides the strength to keep the carcass from racking. The framing for a frameless cabinet is shown in **3-6**. The doors and drawers fit as shown in **3-7**. The vanity in **3-8** is frameless, with the doors and drawers fitting over the edges of the bulkheads.

3-8 A typical frameless vanity with the doors and drawers overlaying the edges of the bulkheads.

DOORS

Raised panel doors are widely used on quality bathroom cabinets. The door has a frame of solid wood composed of stiles and rails. The panels are usually solid-wood strips edge glued and machined on the edges (**3-9**). The vanity in **3-5** has doors of this type. Some cabinets use doors and drawer fronts made from medium-density fiberboard (MDF) with a hardwood or plastic laminate bonded to it. The raised panel is molded in the MDF. Another type of MDF door is coated with a polyvinyl (PVC) coating that is then painted.

DRAWERS

Drawers are constructed to be used on cabinets with faceframes or frameless units in the same manner as described for doors. Review **3-4** and **3-7**.

Drawer sides may be hardwood, particleboard, plywood, or hardboard. The bottoms may be hardboard or plywood. The drawer sides are connected to the drawer front with dovetails or stapled, nailed, or screwed (**3-10**).

For best results drawers should run on steel glides with nylon rollers (**3-11**). They can be run on wood glides but these tend to stick and the drawer will not track as smoothly.

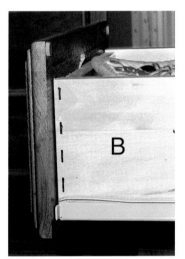

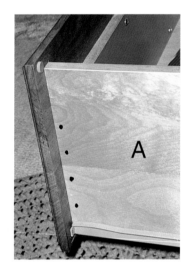

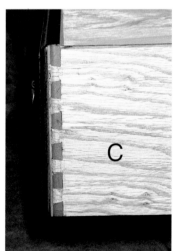

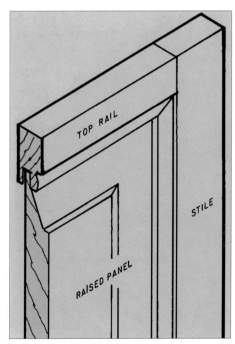

3-9 Typical panel door construction.

3-10 Drawer fronts are usually connected to the sides with dovetails, nails, staples, or screws. Drawer A has nails, B staples, and C is dovetailed.

3-11 Metal drawer glides provide the best way to install a drawer. They give smooth performance and will carry heavier loads than wood glides.

CARCASS MATERIALS

The cabinet carcass is typically made with plywood or particleboard. Plywood carcasses have a natural wood veneer bonded on the exposed surface. Particleboard panels may be covered with a vinyl or paper film that has a wood-grain image or a solid color. These are not durable. A low-pressure laminate made of a paper layer saturated with a melamine resin is better. The most durable exterior covering is a high-pressure laminate. It will resist damage from things hitting it. High-pressure laminates are made by bonding multiple layers of resin-impregnated paper fused together under heat and pressure to form a hard, durable sheet.

HARDWARE

Hinges may be concealed or visible. A concealed hinge is shown in **3-12**. It is mounted on the inside of the door and the cabinet. Another type is shown in **3-13**. Notice the slot in the cabinet mounting that permits adjustment of the door.

There are many types of decorative hinge that are partially exposed. A typical barrel-type decorative hinge is in **3-14**. All that shows is the decorative barrel. There are many variations of exposed hinges available.

Some hinges are self-closing. They hold the door open and when closed keep pressure on it to stay closed so you do not need a cabinet door catch. If you decide to use a door catch consider using a magnetic catch. It gives less of a problem than the spring-type catches.

The choice of door and drawer handles and pulls is extensive. They should be compatible with the hinges, cabinet design, and other accessories in the bath.

Courtesy Julius Blum, Inc.

3-12 A concealed hinge mounts on the inside of the door and cabinet. This hinge has a lever permitting you to remove the door.

3-13 This small concealed hinge mounts on the inside of the door and around the faceframe.

3-14 A typical exposed barrel decorative hinge.

ACCESSORIES

As you visit showrooms of plumbing fixture dealers notice the wide range of accessories they have available. Look through magazines related to homes and those featuring home products. As you lay out the bathroom and choose and locate the fixtures always keep in mind the accessories you want or need. Following are some that are required and others that are nice to have available.

A medicine cabinet is a shallow cabinet stored between the studs. It usually has mirrored doors. They are available as a single door (**3-15**) or multiple-door units (**3-16**) usually with mirrors on the doors. The doors are a little larger than the case and close flat against the wall. Single-door medicine cabinets are made to fit between studs spaced 16 inches O.C. This space is 14½ inches wide. The typical wood stud is 3½ inches deep and the medicine cabinet is sized to fit into this shallow opening. If you have two- or three-door medicine cabinets you will have to cut one or more studs and install a header and sill forming the rough opening for the cabinet (**3-17**). Have one door locked to keep medicines secure from children.

If you are remodeling and are going to install a medicine cabinet, carefully remove some of the dry wall in the area. Look for electric wires or plumbing before doing a major tearout.

Cabinets are available with hinged and sliding doors. The sliding doors always cover half the cabinet and can be bothersome. Some cabinets are deeper than the 3½-inch stud depth and will protrude a bit beyond the wall. This causes no problem and does give additional depth. Be certain the swinging doors do not strike some other accessory as a drinking glass holder.

Another type of small cabinet is sized much like the medicine cabinet but is mounted with its back against the wall (**3-18**). It is typically around 4 inches deep and causes no problem protruding into the room.

Mirrors are another required accessory. As just mentioned if you install a medicine cabinet you will most likely have a small mirror. It is popular to install a mirror over the lavatory and make it run from the backsplash 36 inches or higher up the wall and the entire length of the lavatory cabinet (**3-19**). Small plate-glass mirrors are typically 3/16 or ¼ inch thick. Consider using the thicker mirror.

In a large master bathroom consider mounting a 24 × 48 to 60-inches-long mirror vertically on a door or the wall. This enables you to view your outfit from head to toe.

3-15 This single-door medicine cabinet is recessed into the wall. Notice the decorative double-layer mirror.

3-16 This recessed medicine cabinet is totally wood. Each door opens giving access to one-third of the interior.

Courtesy Crane Plumbing/Flat Products/Universal-Rundle

CONSTRUCTING BATHROOMS

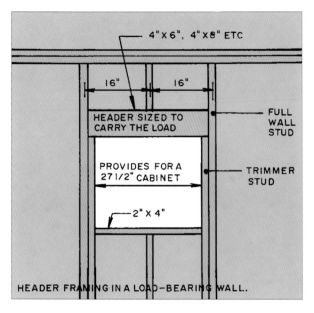

4"×6", 4"×8" ETC

16"　16"

HEADER SIZED TO
CARRY THE LOAD

FULL
WALL
STUD

PROVIDES FOR A
27 1/2" CABINET

TRIMMER
STUD

2"×4"

HEADER FRAMING IN A LOAD—BEARING WALL.

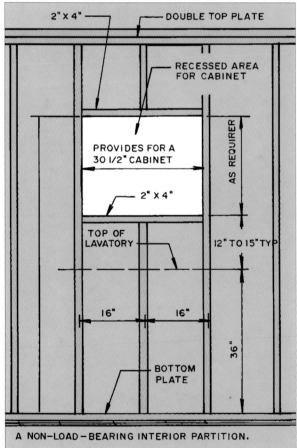

2"×4"　DOUBLE TOP PLATE

RECESSED AREA
FOR CABINET

PROVIDES FOR A
30 1/2" CABINET

AS REQUIRER

2"×4"

TOP OF
LAVATORY

12" TO 15" TYP

16"　16"

36"

BOTTOM
PLATE

A NON—LOAD—BEARING INTERIOR PARTITION.

3-17 (Top and bottom) Typical wall framing for a
recessed medicine cabinet on an interior wall.

3-18 The back of this cabinet is mounted flush to
the wall.

3-19 This custom-made double lavatory cabinet has
a full-length plate-glass mirror.

A wall-hung mirror with a shelf below is a good way to get an extra mirror in a room or over a small lavatory (**3-20**).

Towel bars, hooks, and rings are used for hanging towels and washcloths. They are available in many styles and several finishes (**3-21** and **3-22**). Select these to go with the medicine cabinet, fixtures, and the color of the walls and floor. Place larger bars near the shower and tub to carry the large bath towels. Place smaller bars, hooks, or rings near the lavatory to carry hand towels. One near the toilet and bidet is also helpful. Study the location of these accessories in **3-23**.

The height to place these accessories can vary depending upon the situation. In general the towel bars, rings, and hooks are placed 48 inches above the floor and 15 to 20 inches from the shower or tub.

Soap holders are placed at the lavatory (**3-21**). They are usually built in fiberglass tubs and showers. If you have a custom-built shower with tile walls, soap holders the size of a tile are available and are installed in place of a tile.

Drinking glass holders are placed in the lavatory area (**3-21**). Some companies make toothbrush holders.

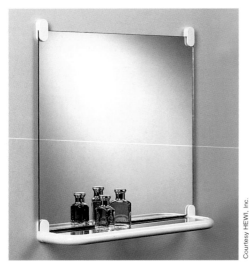

3-20 This wall-hung mirror has a shelf made from nylon below it adding extra convenience.

3-21 This towel ring, drinking glass holder, and soap dish are accessories used in the sink area. Notice the shelf below the mirror. These are made of nylon and available in several colors.

3-22 Metal towel hooks, bars, and rings are available in various colored finishes.

To hang your robe, pajamas, or other clothing you can install **robe hooks** wherever there is a convenient wall. Place it high enough above the floor so garments do not drag on it. A **clothes tree** is also a useful accessory if you have room in an open corner.

Of course you need a **toilet tissue dispenser**. It is located as shown in Chapter 1. You may want a **paper tissue holder**. It holds an entire box of tissues and is more attractive than letting the box sit on the lavatory or the toilet tank. A **waste basket** is essential and should be able to hold moist tissues and cloths. You may want to plan a space for a **scale** if you weigh yourself frequently. Otherwise it can be placed in a storage cabinet that gives easy access.

Courtesy HEWI, Inc.

3-23 This sink area has the convenience of a towel bar, a shelf, drinking glass holder, soap dish, a hook holding washcloths, and a waste receptacle.

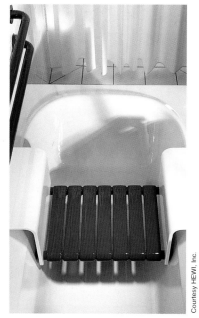

ACCESSORIES FOR A BARRIER-FREE BATHROOM

Accessories for helping those with physical limitations are available. In **3-24** is a seat that can be installed in a shower, and a tub seat is in **3-25**. Grab bars and a shower seat that will fold up out of the way are shown in **3-26**. A completely barrier-free shower is seen in **3-27**. The floor is flush with the floor of the room. Curtains are used instead of walls, permitting a wheelchair user to enter. This installation has nylon accessories to carry the curtain, hold a seat, a shelf for holding small items, and a showerhead installation.

3-24 This nylon shower seat is mounted on the shower wall. It will fold up when not needed.

3-25 A bathtub seat is a great safety accessory and enables a person with limited strength or mobility to bathe. Notice the grab bars on the wall.

3-26 A barrier-free shower and tub installation with the required grab bars, seats, and showerhead. These are all nylon accessories.

3-27 This is a barrier-free shower with a variety of nylon accessories.

3-28 These nylon grab bars provide the security needed by the toilet as required by the Americans With Disabilities Act.

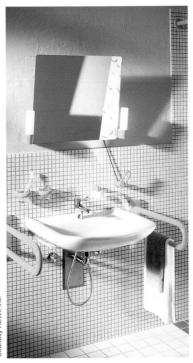

3-29 This wall-hung lavatory has nylon gripping rails on each side.

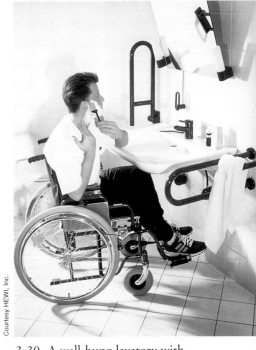

3-30 A wall-hung lavatory with nylon gripping rails provides barrier-free access to the fixture.

A wall-hung toilet with wall-mounted support rails is in **3-28**. These are as required by the Americans With Disabilities Act. It has a 36-inch grab bar on the adjacent wall. Similar rails for gripping are installed on each side of a wall-hung lavatory (**3-29**). The leg area under the lavatory permits a wheelchair user to have easy access to the fixture (**3-30**). A complete barrier-free bathroom is shown in **3-31**.

3-31 A complete barrier-free bathroom uses carefully selected fixtures and accessories enabling those with physical limitations to access the fixtures with a minimum of difficulty.

CABINETS, COUNTERTOPS & ACCESSORIES

Courtesy Formica Corporation

3-32 High-pressure plastic laminate is an inexpensive, durable, moisture-resistant countertop material.

3-33 The edge of the countertop can be bonded with a wood strip that matches the cabinet wood. It must have a durable, moisture-resistant finish.

3-34 Plastic laminate countertops are generally banded with plastic laminate strips. A slight dark line shows along the edge when it is trimmed.

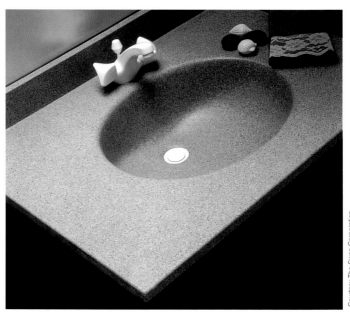

Courtesy The Swan Corporation

3-35 This solid surface-molded countertop is impact resistant, resists damage from heat and cold, and is easily cleaned. This lavatory top has the bowl, countertop, and backsplash molded into a seamless single unit.

COUNTERTOPS

There are a number of materials that can be used for bathroom lavatory countertops. Natural materials such as granite and marble are heavy and expensive. Cutting and fitting requires the services of professional stone cutters. Marble tends to stain and chip and is not a good choice.

PLASTIC LAMINATES

High-pressure plastic laminates are probably the most widely used materials. They are made of several layers of kraft paper impregnated with phenolic resins and a layer of translucent colored or printed paper on top treated with a melamine resin. They are available in many colors and patterns, clean easily, resist wear and moisture. They can be damaged if hit by something sharp (3-32). They wear well, are water-resistant, and are easy to clean.

The laminate is easily cut and shaped. It is bonded to the plywood or particleboard top with contact cement. The wood top should be at least ¾ inch thick. It may be installed butting a wood edge (3-33) or by bonding plastic laminate to the edge (3-34). When bonding it to the edge, you will get a dark edge showing where the laminate has been trimmed to size.

SOLID SYNTHETIC MATERIALS

There are a number of synthetic countertop materials. They are a cast plastic resin such as acrylic, polyester, or a combination of these and mineral fillers. They have the advantage of having the color completely through the material. They are waterproof and resist stain, heat, and scratches. However, take care and do not abuse them. Some types have a special compound you can use to repair chips. Minor scratches can be buffed or lightly sanded out because the color goes all the way through the material. They are available in a variety of solid colors, granite-like material, and other patterns. Solid-surface coun-

tertop materials are more expensive than high-pressure plastic laminates but less expensive than granite or marble.

One such product is the Swanstone® molded solid-surface countertop shown in 3-35. This seamless molded-edge countertop is sold in lengths and is cut and installed with existing tools. It is impact resistant, resists damage from heat and cold, and cleans with normal detergent. Scratches can be buffed out with a fine steelwool or abrasive paper. It is available with a splashback bonded to the wall or a molded coved splashback as shown in 3-36. The top seen in 3-35 has the lavatory bowl, countertop, and backsplash in a single, seamless, molded unit.

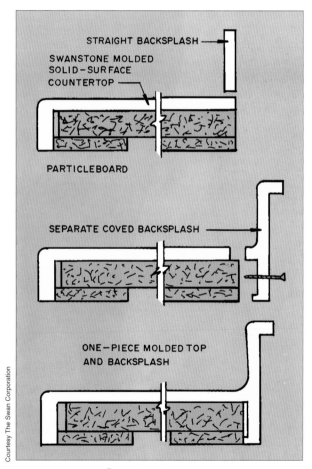

Courtesy The Swan Corporation

3-36 Swanstone® solid-surface countertops have several types of backsplash.

Another solid surfacing material is Surell®, manufactured by Formica Corporation. This is a solid, dense resin and mineral composite that has a smooth outer finish. It has a range of colors and patterns. One example is shown in **3-37**. The colors and pattern run all the way through the material.

3-37 Surell® is a solid surfacing countertop material made using a dense resin and natural minerals. The color runs all the way through the material.

Avonite® is another solid-surfacing material used on countertops, furniture, wall cladding, and for other architectural purposes where a waterproof and durable material is needed. It is a patented, composite, non-porous material that has the color throughout its entire thickness. It is available in either polyester or acrylic. It is also formed into sinks as shown in **3-38**.

Cultured marble is a product made from marble chips and dust cast into a polyester resin. It has a thin gelcoat surface. The more expensive countertops have a thicker gelcoat that helps resist crazing and cracking. The sink bowl and countertop are cast as a single unit so there are no seams (**3-39**). The gelcoat surface is not as resistant to damage as other materials but works well in bathroom applications.

CERAMIC TILE COUNTERTOPS

Ceramic tile countertops are hard, tough, and resistant to damage from heat. When properly installed with the correct grout, they resist moisture penetration. An epoxy grout seems to work well for bathroom tile countertops.

3-38 Avonite® solid-surfacing material is used for surfacing countertops and is formed into sinks.

There are a great variety and abundance of choices available for tiles. You can use either floor or wall tiles which are available in a wide choice of colors and patterns. The cost varies quite a bit depending upon the tile chosen and whether it has been imported (**3-40**).

3-39 This is a cultured-marble bathroom lavatory and countertop that has been cast as a single unit. It does not stain and is easy to keep clean.

Courtesy American Standard, Inc.

3-40 This vitreous china self-rimming countertop lavatory is set into a tile countertop providing a durable and beautiful installation.

While tile can be bonded directly to a plywood or particleboard countertop substrate, this is not recommended. If the grout fails, moisture will get below the tile, causing the wood to swell and the tile to work loose. The tile should be set on a cement board secured to the wood top or on a bed of mortar as shown in **3-41**. The tile is usually placed on the wall up to the bottom of the mirror or medicine cabinet.

OTHER LAVATORY COUNTERTOPS

The manufacturers of bath fixtures have available a number of very beautiful and creative lavatories. The one in **3-42** has a glass bowl mounted in a glass top. The bowl and top are very durable and easy to keep clean.

MIRROR OR MEDICINE CABINET

NOTE: COVER THE CEMENT BOARD SEAMS WITH FIBERGLASS TAPE SET IN THE ADHESIVE.

TILE THE WALL UP TO THE MIRROR OR MEDICINE CABINET

GYPSUM WALLBOARD

WATERPROOF MEMBRANE AND TILE ADHESIVE

LATEX-PORTLAND CEMENT MORTAR

COVE TILE

CERAMIC TILE

CERAMIC COUNTERTOP EDGE

WALL STUD

EXTERIOR PLYWOOD

CEMENTITIOUS BOARD

HARDWOOD NOSING TO MATCH CABINETS

ALTERNATE NOSING

3-41 Typical installation detail for ceramic tile countertop and wall backsplash.

Courtesy Jacuzzi Whirlpool Bath

3-42 This glass lavatory bowl set in a glass countertop gives a unique and attractive feature to the bathroom. The materials are durable and completely moisture resistant.

Another approach is to use a high-fired vitreous china, triple-glazed pedestal lavatory. It does not require a countertop so accessory shelves or a small cabinet are used to hold things (**3-43**).

Courtesy Jacuzzi Whirlpool Bat

3-43 This pedestal lavatory is made from a vitreous china heavily glazed. It is very durable and will serve for many years. It does not require a cabinet base or a countertop.

Bathroom Fixtures

One of the first things you will do after making your preliminary decisions about what you want in the bathroom is to start getting information about the fixtures that are available. As you visit local dealers and examine the products in their showrooms, you can expect to get some new ideas. You likely will want to revise your preliminary plan. Take copies of their brochures because these also show fixtures that may not be on display. Brochures will also let you take home photos showing the colors available. All of this is necessary as you make final decisions on which fixtures to use and the color scheme for the bathroom.

4-1 Selecting attractively designed fixtures, working them into a comfortable arrangement, and giving careful attention to color will allow you to create a bathroom beyond the typical and merely serviceable.

Possibly the first thing you will notice is the great variety of fixture shapes, sizes, and colors that are available. This gives you the opportunity to create a bathroom that is more attractive and functional than what has been typical in residential construction (4-1). As you consider the fixtures remember to select the accessories to be used with them. Again there is a variety of designs and materials available.

MATERIALS

Vitreous china is a ceramic material that has a vitreous (glass-like) coating on the surface. The fixture is fired in a kiln producing the glazed surface (4-2). While it is excellent for lavatories its major use is in toilets because moisture absorption is almost nonexistent.

Enameled steel, referred to as **porcelain-on-steel**, has a glass-like glaze fused to the steel fixture in a high-temperature kiln. Once widely used for lavatories and tubs, it generally has been replaced by other materials. It does dent and chip.

Enameled cast iron is a porcelain-on-cast-iron product used on lavatories and tubs. It is a good product but the fixtures are very heavy. If you ever need to replace an old cast-iron tub you can smash it into pieces with a sledgehammer.

Synthetic materials consisting of composites made from polyester or acrylics and natural minerals have the color through the entire thickness of the material. They are available in a range of colors and can be cut and drilled with normal woodworking tools. Detailed information is in Chapter 3, on pages 47 and 48. They are widely used for countertops and lavatories.

Cultured marble and **cultured onyx** are often referred to as cast polymers. Cultured marble is a composite of marble chips, marble dust, and a polyester resin. Cultured onyx is a composite of calcareous (porous limestone) and a polyester resin. Cultured marble is opaque whereas cultured onyx has a deep, rich color. These materials are used to cast countertops and lavatories. Typically the countertop and lavatory are cast as a single piece.

4-2 This vitreous china lavatory sink has a glass-like finish and is impervious to moisture and easy to clean.

Courtesy American Standard, Inc.

Acrylics and fiberglass are used to produce tubs, showers, and whirlpools. These are made in a number of ways. For example, the fixture could be molded of acrylic or ABS (acrilonitrite butadiene styrene) and then sprayed with fiberglass to strengthen the shell (4-3). ABS and acrylic produce a durable gelcoat. Some fixtures may be molded of fiberglass that is sprayed into a mold that has been coated with a gelcoat. New products of this nature are occasionally developed so you need to be certain what you are buying. Which is the least likely to crack or deteriorate with age?

Courtesy Eljer Plumbingware Inc.

4-3 This sculptured whirlpool has 14 jets and a built-in seat. It is made of acrylic reinforced with fiberglass.

Courtesy Avonite, Inc.

4-4 This lavatory is made from polyester resins and natural fillers. It is durable and impervious to moisture. It is mounted below the top.

Following are examples of some of the fixtures available including some amenities such as choosing a whirlpool, sauna, or bidet.

LAVATORIES

Lavatories are available made from vitreous china, enameled steel, or cast iron, solid synthetic composite materials, and glass. The types available include drop-in, wall hung, pedestal, and integral.

Drop-in lavatories are set into an opening cut in the countertop. They may be mounted on top of the countertop, from below, or set flush with it. The drop-in lavatory in 4-4 is mounted from below the countertop. It is made from a synthetic composite. Typical mounting techniques are shown in 4-5.

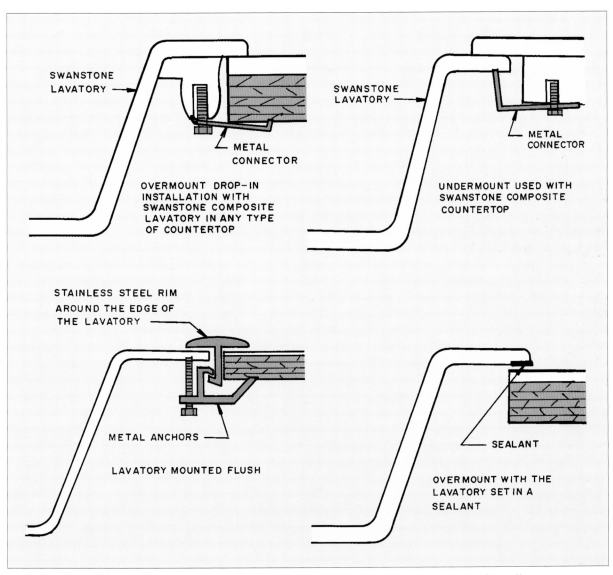

SWANSTONE LAVATORY

METAL CONNECTOR

OVERMOUNT DROP-IN INSTALLATION WITH SWANSTONE COMPOSITE LAVATORY IN ANY TYPE OF COUNTERTOP

SWANSTONE LAVATORY

METAL CONNECTOR

UNDERMOUNT USED WITH SWANSTONE COMPOSITE COUNTERTOP

STAINLESS STEEL RIM AROUND THE EDGE OF THE LAVATORY

METAL ANCHORS

LAVATORY MOUNTED FLUSH

SEALANT

OVERMOUNT WITH THE LAVATORY SET IN A SEALANT

4-5 Lavatories are mounted in vanity tops in any of several ways. Consider the method of installation as you choose the lavatories for your bathroom.

4-6 This round glass lavatory bowl is kiln-fired to provide superior durability. It adds a special and colorful feature to a bathroom.

An extraordinary colored-glass lavatory set into a clear-glass countertop is shown in **4-6**. A fixture like this will add some interest to the overall appearance of your bathroom.

Wall-hung lavatories are bolted to the wall with metal brackets. Special blocking is inserted between the studs to carry the load. They have the advantage of providing open floor area below. This is very helpful in small bathroom where wheelchair users will be using the bathroom.

Pedestal lavatories occupy a minimum of space, and since there is no cabinet do not crowd the open floor area as much as a lavatory mounted on a base cabinet. Wall-hung units have the same advantage and do not have the pedestal base to get in the way. The pedestal bowl is available in a number of shapes and sizes (**4-7**). It does not have a backsplash so the wall is usually tiled. Be careful you do not crowd the lavatory into too narrow a space. You should consider keeping it 15 inches off a wall and allow a 30-inch wall space. Wall-hung units need the same spacing.

A lovely pedestal lavatory is shown in **4-8**. The use of a glass bowl, top, and base provides an attractive feature in a bathroom.

4-7 This is a large pedestal lavatory providing some horizontal surface area to hold your soap, toothbrush, and other articles. Notice the wall is tiled providing a backsplash. It is a vitreous china fixture.

4-8 This pedestal lavatory has a glass bowl, top, and base. It is a European designed and imported fixture.

Courtesy American Standard, Inc.

4-9 Cultured-marble lavatory and countertops are cast as a single unit. Therefore there are no cracks, so keeping it clean is easy.

Courtesy Avonite, Inc.

4-10 This lavatory bowl and countertop are made from synthetic materials and formed as a single piece.

Integral lavatories have the bowl and countertop cast in one piece. The materials used include synthetic composites, cultured marble, and cultured onyx. The entire unit is secured to the vanity. Stock sizes are available to fit stock vanities. However, custom sizes can be made. Some synthetic composites can be cut to length on the site. A cultured marble lavatory and countertop are shown in **4-9**. The backsplash is also cultured marble. An integral top and bowl made of a synthetic composite are shown in **4-10**. Notice this installation fits between walls. The top can be cut to make a perfect fit.

TOILETS

Toilets have changed a great deal over the past few years and, before you make a final selection, visit your local plumbing fixture dealer and get a review of the current most efficient fixtures available. Seek advice on which toilets have proven to be most effective and have caused the least trouble. Then talk with your plumber. Find out the types and brands he/she would recommend.

In the 1980s residential toilets used gravity flow, required five or six gallons of water per flush, and had a water circle area of around 8 × 8 inches. When concern about our water supply increased, more efficient units were developed. Some required only 3.5 gallons per flush. If you are remodeling, you will most likely have one of these toilets which no longer are acceptable and it will have to be replaced by a more efficient unit. These are low-consumption units that use 1.6 gallons per flush (**4-11**). This is the standard set by the U.S. federal government. This standard requires all toilets installed after January 1, 1994, to meet the 1.6 gallon requirement. Some manufacturers are even producing toilets using only one gallon per flush.

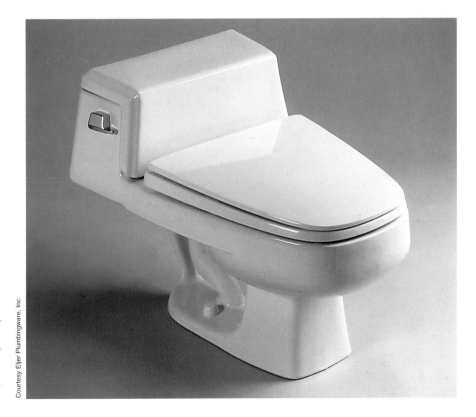

Courtesy Eljer Plumbingware, Inc.

4-11 This one-piece toilet is often called a low-profile toilet. It uses 1.6 gallons per flush and is made from vitreous china.

BASIC TYPES OF TOILET

Toilets are available in three basic types. **One-piece toilets** are cast so that the tank and bowl are a single unit (**4-12**). The tank is usually very low. The second type is a **two-piece unit** that has the tank and bowl as separate pieces. The tank is bolted to the back of the bowl (**4-13**). This is probably the most frequently used type. A third type has a small **wall-mounted tank** that is 5 or 6 feet above the bowl. It is only used if you are trying to reproduce the appearance of an old-fashioned bathroom.

Toilets vary in size, but typically fall within the sizes shown in **4-14**, **4-15**, and **4-16**.

GRAVITY-FED & PRESSURIZED TOILETS

The current efficient toilets are either **gravity-fed** or **pressurized**. Plumbing standards require a single flush to move a flow at least 40 feet along the waste line. While this may be available with the gravity-fed 1.6 gallon toilet, sometimes a second flush is necessary. Flow in the waste line from the tub, shower, and lavatory help keep the waste moving. Pressure-assisted toilets usually have enough pressure to move the flow 60 feet down the waste line. They have a pressure capsule with a valve in the tank that fills with air when the toilet is flushed. As the tank fills, water

4-12 This is a one-piece toilet using a siphon-jet flushing system.

4-13 A two-piece toilet that has the tank made separate and has it bolted to the back of the bowl.

partially fills this capsule putting the air remaining under pressure. When flushed this air helps push the water into the trap and pushes the waste with more than the force of gravity. This enables the toilet to use less than the 1.6 gallon standard for gravity-fed toilets. Pressurized toilets cost considerably more than the gravity-fed type and are noisier.

BIDETS

A bidet looks like a small toilet or urinal. It is used for personal hygience in the pelvic area. A bidet is typically 15 inches high and extends out from the wall 22 to 26 inches (4-17). It has a cold and hot water supply and a drain. The water is supplied by a spray that may be on the

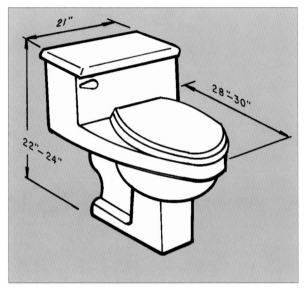

4-14 Typical size of a one-piece standard toilet.

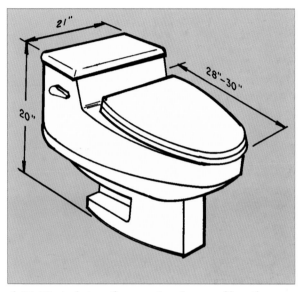

4-15 Typical size of a one-piece low-profile toilet.

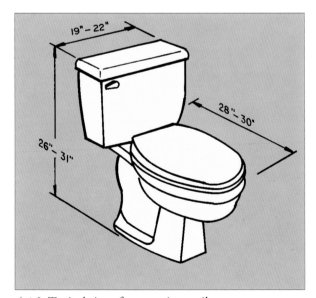

4-16 Typical size of a two-piece toilet.

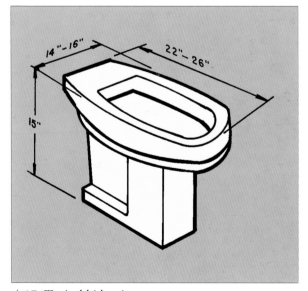

4-17 Typical bidet size.

bottom or back of the bowl. Bidets are usually installed next to the toilet (**4-18**). They are made in the same style as the toilet and you should choose one the same color. Be certain to leave sufficient room between it and the toilet. Normally it needs a 30-inch clear wall space.

BATHTUBS

Bathtubs are available in enameled steel, enameled cast iron, acrylic, fiberglass with a gel coat or an acrylic coating, and ABS. The shapes and sizes vary depending upon the manufacturer, but the most commonly used are shown in **4-19**. The colors available match the toilets, showers, and lavatories made by the same company.

4-18 A bidet is usually placed next to the toilet.

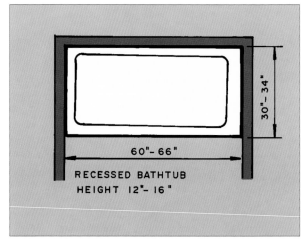

RECESSED BATHTUB
HEIGHT 12"- 16"

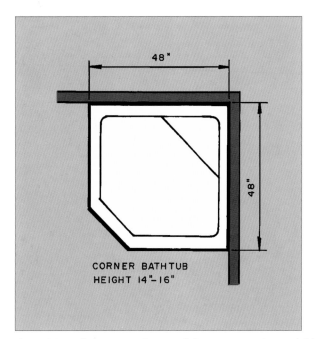

CORNER BATHTUB
HEIGHT 14"-16"

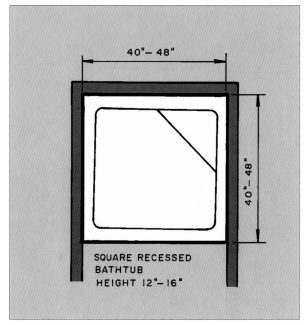

SQUARE RECESSED BATHTUB
HEIGHT 12"-16"

4-19 Typical shapes and sizes of three commonly available bathtubs.

Some bathtubs are designed to fit between two walls and only have a finished front side (4-20). A **recessed acrylic bathtub** is shown in 4-21. A bathtub such as this set in a recess can have the walls and tub made of acrylic or fiberglass as a single unit. There are no seams between the tub and wall.

4-20 This bathtub has only a finished front side. The open ends will butt the walls in a recessed area.

4-21 This acrylic bathtub is set in a recess between walls. The wall covering is an integral part of the tub.

Some bathtubs are made to be placed in the center of the room and are finished on all four sides. These are referred to as **freestanding units**. One way to build these is to use a **platform**. This is a wood framework, forming a platform usually about 12 inches high. The bathtub has no sides but is set in an opening in the top of the platform.

The sides can be ceramic tile, synthetic composites, or wood paneling and the top can be any of the materials used for countertops (**4-22**). The platform installation in **4-23** is set between end walls so it only has one side exposed. The bathtub has a rounded, sculptured design adding to the overall attractiveness of the bathroom.

Courtesy American Standard, Inc.

4-22
A platform bathtub has the tub set in the top of the platform. This two-step platform is finished with ceramic tile.

Courtesy American Standard, Inc.

4-23 This platform installation is set between end walls. Notice the freshness added by the natural light. The bathtub has a sculptured design setting it apart from the typical flat rectangular bathtub.

Courtesy American Standard, Inc.

4-24 This free-form bathtub illustrates the special designs available from some manufacturers. It brings a refreshing appearance to a bathroom.

Manufacturers produce a number of special bathtubs that carry the design beyond the typical product. One such unit is in **4-24**. This free-form bathtub is not only attractive but will fit into a relatively small space.

If you are remodeling be certain you can get the old bathtub out the door and the new one into the room. Sometimes a bit of carpentry is needed to remove the doorframe and a stud or two. If you have to make a turn getting the tub down a hall or up a stair, check this out. Acrylic and fiberglass bathtubs are lighter than metal ones and may be a good choice if difficult handling is necessary. Remember to check the location of the hot and cold water lines and the waste pipe. Move them before you set the tub in the room.

WHIRLPOOL TUBS & SPAS

A whirlpool tub is filled with water for each use. It has many jets operated by a pump. The jets produce streams of water across your body, helping you to relax and ease tension. After you are finished, you drain the water away in the same manner as a bathtub.

Whirlpools are made from the same materials as bathtubs. They are available in a variety of sizes and shapes, from typical rectangular to very popular oval shapes. They usually are sized to hold two or more people. A range of colors is also available, so they can add to the appearance of the bathroom (**4-25**).

4-25 This whirlpool installation has the colors coordinated with the lavatory and other fixtures. The oval shape is very popular.

Courtesy Aqua Glass Corporation

A freestanding whirlpool built into a platform is shown in **4-26**. This is a large unit and requires a large bathroom, but the beauty makes the space worthwhile. The whirlpool in **4-27** is built into a recess in the wall and only requires one side to have a finished panel.

A spa is larger and deeper than a whirlpool. The water is not drained away but is retained and heated when it is to be used by electric or gas heaters. It is typically installed outdoors on a deck or patio. It was originally made as a wood tub but other materials are now used.

4-26 This large freestanding whirlpool will hold at least two people in spacious comfort. The wood paneling on the platform adds warmth to the room.

CONSTRUCTING BATHROOMS

Courtesy Jacuzzi Whirlpool Bath

Courtesy Crane Plumbing/Flat Products/Universal-Rundle

4-27 This rectangular whirlpool is built into a recess in the wall, This is an efficient way to install such a unit.

4-28 This white whirlpool is set into the floor. The block platform surrounding it gives it a featured appearance.

Another way to install a whirlpool is to set it into an opening in the floor. The unit in **4-28** has a rim of about 6 inches into which the whirlpool was installed. This requires cutting floor joists so some structural design and load-carrying piers below the floor are required.

The triangular whirlpool in **4-29** is designed for installation in a corner. The extended beveled rim in this installation rests on the floor. However, it could be installed on a platform.

Courtesy Jacuzzi Whirlpool Bath

4-29 This unique corner whirlpool has a beveled rim resting on the floor. The tub extends below the floor.

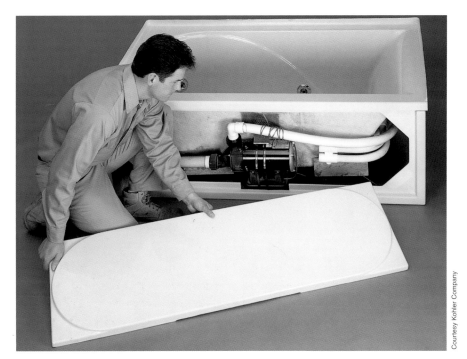

Courtesy Kohler Company

4-30 The pump used to circulate water to the jets is located in the side of the whirlpool.

Courtesy Alumax Bath Enclosures

4-31 This metal-framed glass shower enclosure makes a bathtub serve as a shower whenever one is wanted.

The water jets are nozzles in the sides of the pool. Some are located to hit the body, some the neck, and others the feet. This provides full body relaxation. The water is circulated under pressure by a pump located below the body of the whirlpool (4-30). The hot water circulated is drawn from the residential hot water heater. Some units have an in-line water heater. Be certain when you locate the whirlpool that you arrange to have access to the pump should repairs be needed.

SHOWERS

Showers are possibly the most popular way to bathe. The water temperature can be varied, the soap is washed away, and you feel refreshed from the pressure of the water as it sprays over you.

Every home should at have at least one shower. They are the only way some people with physical limitations can bathe.

Possibly the easiest and least expensive way to get a shower is to mount a showerhead in the wall over a bathtub. With the use of metal and glass enclosures a nice size shower is available (4-31). If you have the room, it is helpful to have a shower separate from the bathtub. A shower stall is easier to use and is safer to use than a tub shower. You might consider having one bath with a bathtub and use only a shower in the second bath.

Showers may be prefabricated units of acrylic or fiberglass having the floor and walls made as a single unit. Some have a seat built into one side (4-32). They are sold with a metal and glass door with gaskets that seal the water inside a prefabricated shower. Remember that one 32-inch

4-32 A prefabricated shower has the walls, floor, and a seat molded into a single unit.

square inside is typically the minimum allowed by most codes. If possible, go to 36- or 48-inch sizes. They are more convenient to use.

If you are remodeling, remember to check whether, or how, you can get the new prefabricated shower into the bathroom. Since they are a large, single unit, they are difficult to maneuver through stairs, halls, and doorways. Some companies make acrylic or fiberglass showers with the walls and pan as separate pieces that are assembled in the bathroom. While you have seams that need to be sealed, this may be the only way you can get a new shower installed without extensive carpentry work.

Custom-built showers are fabricated with pans made from masonry, stone, ceramic tile, acrylics or fiberglass. If you use stone, masonry, or ceramic tile you will have to prepare a waterproof pan typically copper or buy a prefabricated pan made from fiberglass. Using the prefabricated pan simplifies things, but limits the size of the shower to the pan sizes available.

Shower stall pans are available made from acrylic, ceramic, and enameled steel. They are typically 30-, 32-, or 36-inch square bases, 36 × 48 inch rectangular bases, or 36 × 36 inch corner units (4-33).

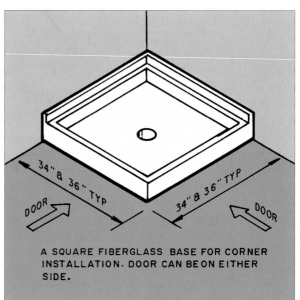

A SQUARE FIBERGLASS BASE FOR CORNER INSTALLATION. DOOR CAN BE ON EITHER SIDE.

4-33 Typical one-piece fiberglass shower pans used with custom-built showers. The walls can be covered with any suitable material. However, ceramic tile is a popular choice.

FIBERGLASS BASE FOR A CORNER SHOWER WITH THE DOOR ON AN ANGLE.

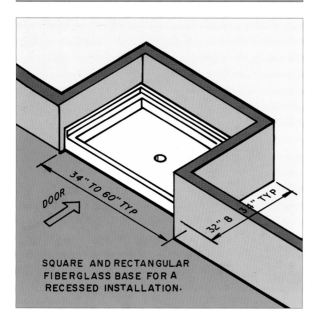

SQUARE AND RECTANGULAR FIBERGLASS BASE FOR A RECESSED INSTALLATION.

CONSTRUCTING BATHROOMS

Shower enclosures are available in kits ready to install. The walls are made from fiberglass or acrylic and can have bi-fold, sliding, or hinged doors. A corner shower with a fiberglass pan and metal-framed glass enclosures on three sides is shown in **4-34**.

4-34
This corner shower uses a fiberglass pan and is enclosed on three sides by a metal-framed glass enclosure assuring a water-tight unit.

Courtesy Alumax Bath Enclosures

Courtesy American Olean Tile Company

The ceramic tile walls in a custom-built shower are enhanced by adding a decorative tile molding about five feet above the floor, as shown in **4-35**. Ceramic soap and shampoo bottle niches are available.

The wall can be covered with metal lath and a bed of cement-sand mortar applied over it to provide a good base for installing the tile. You can also use a cement backerboard composed of a fiberglass-mesh reinforced concrete panel that is not affected by water or water vapor.

A custom-built shower with tile walls on three sides is shown in **4-36**. This has the advantage of being much larger than standard prefabricated units and, with the metal-framed glass enclosures, it is an attractive feature.

4-35 Ceramic tile is widely used on the walls of custom-built showers. It provides a decorative, hard water-resistant wall covering.

Courtesy Alumax Bath Enclosures

4-36 The bronze-framed doors stand out against the black tile walls, presenting an attractive shower installation. This is a recessed installation.

A most interesting custom-built shower is shown in **4-37**. The floor is tile set in a copper pan. The walls are made of glass blocks. Manufactured glass enclosures completes the two open sides. Notice the red column supporting multiple showerheads.

4-37
This striking shower shows how you can use manufactured glass enclosures and water-resistant materials on the floor and walls to create an unusual installation.

Courtesy Alumax Bath Enclosures

Designing the Bathroom Layout

As suggested in Chapter 1, make a list of things you want in the bath and possible uses. Note what questions are raised by this list that you have not yet answered. Follow this list as you select the fixtures and begin to make the layout. If it is in a new house that is still in the design stages, you may be able to change the size and shape of the bathroom and adjacent spaces at this time (5-1). Work until you have answers for each item on your list.

If you are remodeling an existing bath and the room size will not change, make a scale drawing showing the interior dimension. Then locate the fixtures by their centerline, mark the hot and cold water faucets, locate the waste lines, heat outlets, electric outlets, lights, ventilators, doors, and windows (5-2). The symbols used to identify these on drawings are shown in Chapter 6. If you plan to expand the bathroom into the next room or by adding on to the house, show these on the drawing. A typical example is in 5-3. Use a ruler and let every ½ inch represent one foot or use ¼-inch graph paper and let every square represent 6 inches. Measure as accurately as possible.

Courtesy American Standard, Inc.

5-1 If you are designing the bathroom, remember that you need not conform to the usual rectangular shape.

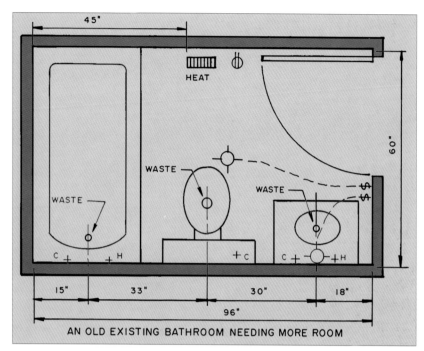

45"

HEAT

WASTE

WASTE

WASTE

60"

C + + H

+ C

C + + H

15"   33"   30"   18"

96"

AN OLD EXISTING BATHROOM NEEDING MORE ROOM

5-2 If you are going to remodel an existing bathroom, first make a dimensioned drawing and locate all utilities and heat outlets.

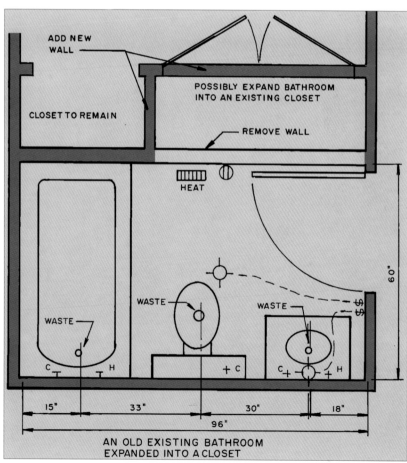

ADD NEW WALL

POSSIBLY EXPAND BATHROOM INTO AN EXISTING CLOSET

CLOSET TO REMAIN

REMOVE WALL

HEAT

WASTE

WASTE

WASTE

60"

C   H

+ C

C +   + H

15"   33"   30"   18"

96"

AN OLD EXISTING BATHROOM
EXPANDED INTO A CLOSET

5-3 If you plan to expand the bathroom into an existing area or by adding on to the house, show this on the original drawing.

DESIGNING THE BATHROOM LAYOUT

If you simply plan to replace the fixtures with new ones in the same location you can use the sizes of the new fixtures to see if they will use the same plumbing and fit into the same place. An easy way to do this is to prepare templates of each new fixture drawn at the same scale as the drawing. You can place them on the drawing and locate space or plumbing problems. The templates are also useful if you plan to relocate fixtures giving an entirely new layout.

If you want a new layout or if it is a new bathroom or one in a house being designed, establish the size of the room and locate proposed doors and windows. Then, using the planning guide-

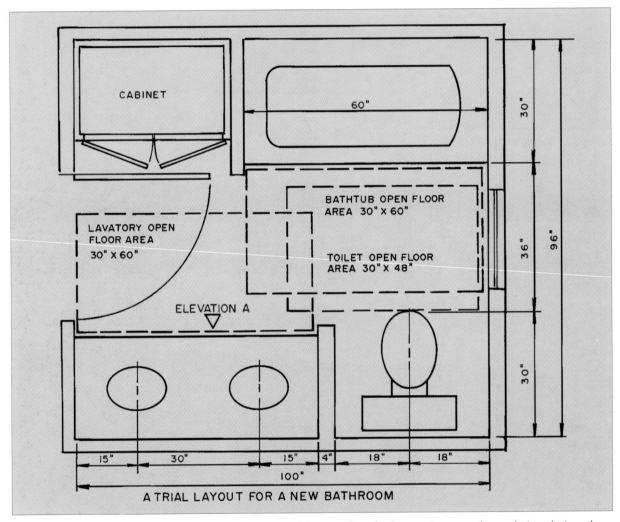

5-4 This layout and that on the opposite page are trial layouts for a bathroom in a new house being designed. At this point you can still change the size and shape of the room because the floor plan has not been finalized.

CONSTRUCTING BATHROOMS

lines in Chapter 2 begin to make some trial layouts (5-4). Since the house exists only on paper you can move the electrical and plumbing features as you wish. Consider making the scale layout as just mentioned and scale templates of each fixture and cabinet you have chosen. Measure the clearances and refer to the guidelines. Consider the flow that allows you to enter the room and allow space to close and open the door. Think back over bathrooms you had in the past and consider things you liked and did not like. Adjust the templates, checking again and again until you reach a satisfactory layout. It is helpful if you lay out the minimum open floor area by each fixture using a dashed line to enclose the area.

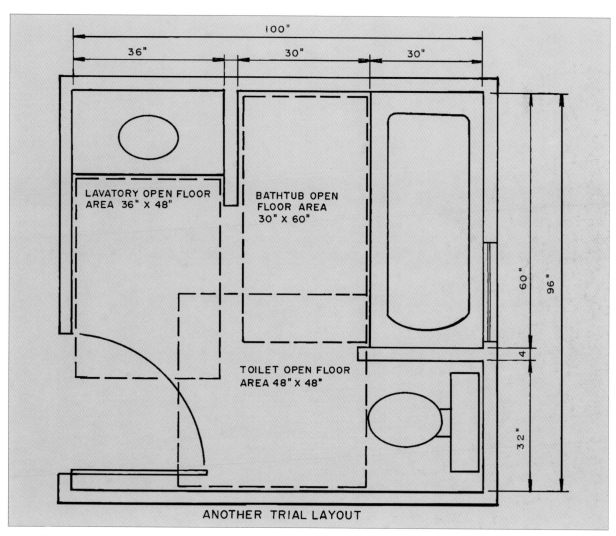

ANOTHER TRIAL LAYOUT

5-4 (Continued)

Once you have reached the final solutions to your layout, make sure the fixtures are carefully located on the drawing. Then you can add up the sizes of the fixtures including the spaces between them. Check whether this adds up to the total length or width of the room.

Should you want to go one step further you could draw an elevation of each wall on graph paper (5-5). Refer to the actual fixture and cabinet sizes and use them as you lay out these drawings. You can indicate accessories as mirrors, wall cabinets, and towel bars.

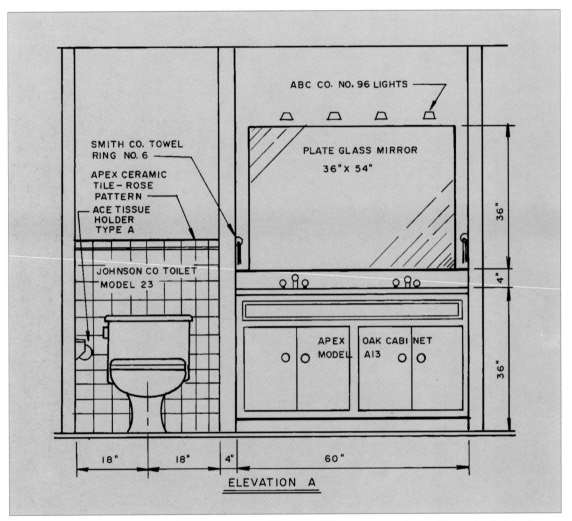

5-5 If you draw an elevation of the bathroom walls you will have a better idea of how the finished room will look.

CONSTRUCTING BATHROOMS

EXPANDING AN EXISTING BATHROOM

If you can handle the extra expense you can expand an existing bathroom by taking over a closet that may be beside it or take a section out of a large room on one side. Earlier, in **5-2**, the bathroom expanded into a bedroom closet. While this helps the bathroom you must have a plan for the lost closet in the bedroom next to it. If it is a very large room you could build anoth-er closet along part of the wall where the original closet was located or use wardrobes to hold clothes that need to be held on hangers.

Another plan that is even more expensive is to add a small addition to the exterior of the house. You must be careful how far out you cantilever (**5-6**) the room, especially if a bathtub or whirl-pool is placed there. The weight must be calcu-lated and the structure designed to hold it. Consider putting a lavatory or toilet on the can-tilever. If the weight is too great you will have to

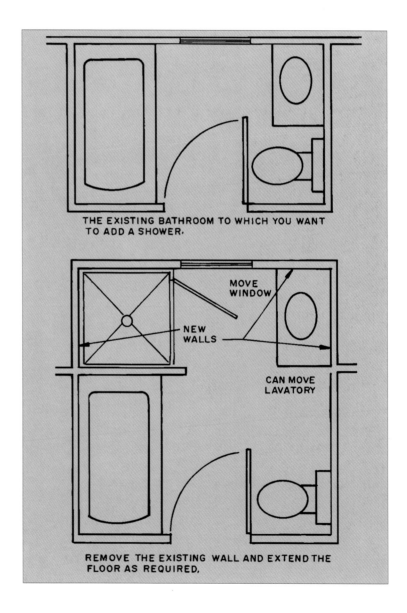

THE EXISTING BATHROOM TO WHICH YOU WANT TO ADD A SHOWER.

MOVE WINDOW

NEW WALLS

CAN MOVE LAVATORY

REMOVE THE EXISTING WALL AND EXTEND THE FLOOR AS REQUIRED.

5-6 You can expand the bathroom by adding a small addition to the outside of the house. This, of course, is rather expensive.

prepare some type of foundation. This can be as simple as using 6 × 6 inch posts to pour a footing and building a masonry wall (5-7). Remember that any water or waste pipes in the area outside the house will freeze unless properly insulated.

SOME MINIMUM LAYOUTS

Following are a number of bathroom layouts that meet minimum standards. These are only a few suggestions and by no means the only possibilities. Observe the planning guidelines in Chapter 2.

Several minimum layouts for a half bath are shown in 5-8. These will typically be below the recommended minimum open floor area. It has a toilet and small lavatory. A key to a successful half bath is the placement of the door. You should be able to enter the bath and close the door without the fixtures getting in your way. You need a clear floor area in which to stand. Swinging the door out is a possible solution.

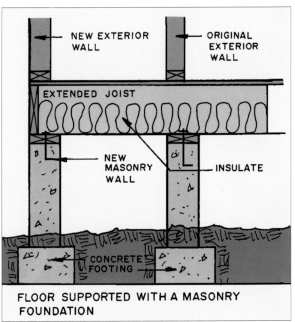

FLOOR SUPPORTED WITH A MASONRY FOUNDATION

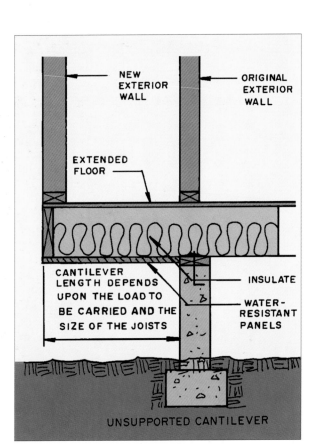

UNSUPPORTED CANTILEVER

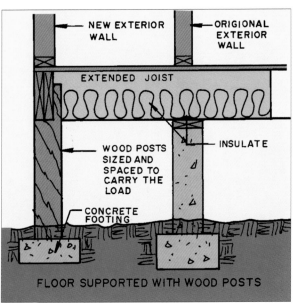

FLOOR SUPPORTED WITH WOOD POSTS

5-7 The expanded section may be a simple cantilever or require support by posts or a masonry foundation.

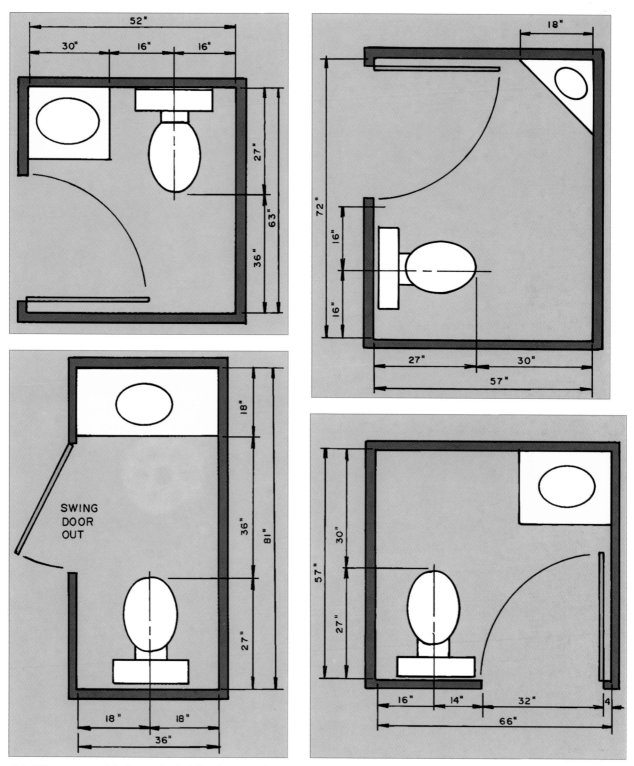

5-8 These are usable but tight half baths (powder rooms) that will function but are below the recommended open floor area. Some designers cut the space in front of the toilet to 24 inches. When you design yours, size it to accept the fixtures you select, and remember to allow for the trim around the door.

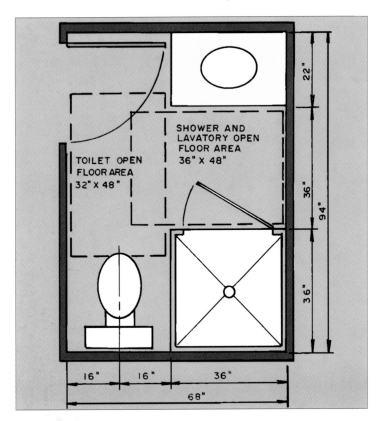

Many second bathrooms have a shower instead of a tub. Several typical minimum layouts are in **5-9**. Observe the minimum clear floor area required for each fixture. These are sometimes referred to as three-quarter bathrooms.

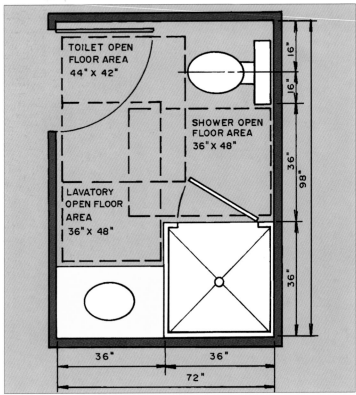

5-9 A three-quarters bath has a shower instead of a tub. It is a good way to have a second or third bathroom.

x

A full bathroom with a tub is the most common type. A shower is built to work in the tub. While this is not as convenient as a separate shower fixture it does make both a tub bath and shower bath available. Several minimum layouts are in **5-10** through **5-14**. The location and swing of the door is a key factor in planning a usable bathroom. You must allow a clear floor space in which to stand that is not intruded upon by the door swing. In very tight, minimum situations consider using a pocket door. It is not as easy to use as a swinging door.

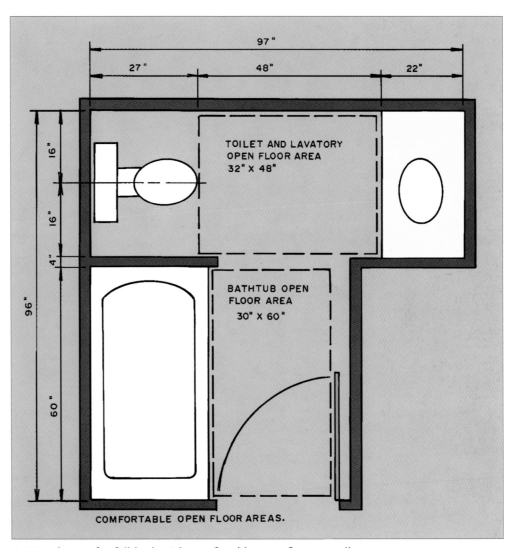

5-10 A layout for full bath with comforatble open floor area allowances. Allow even more open area, whenever possible.

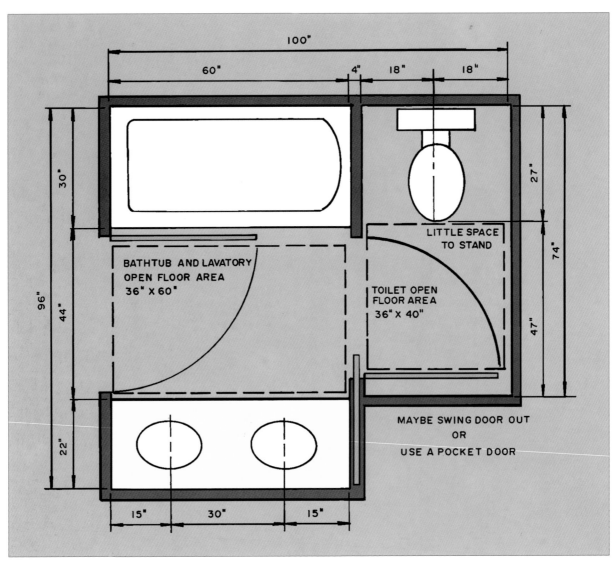

100"

60"   4"   18"   18"

30"

96"   44"

22"

15"   30"   15"

BATHTUB AND LAVATORY
OPEN FLOOR AREA
36" X 60"

LITTLE SPACE
TO STAND

27"

74"

47"

TOILET OPEN
FLOOR AREA
36" X 40"

MAYBE SWING DOOR OUT
OR
USE A POCKET DOOR

5-11 Another layout for full bath. The toilet compartment has a minimum open floor area allowance. Allow more open area, whenever possible.

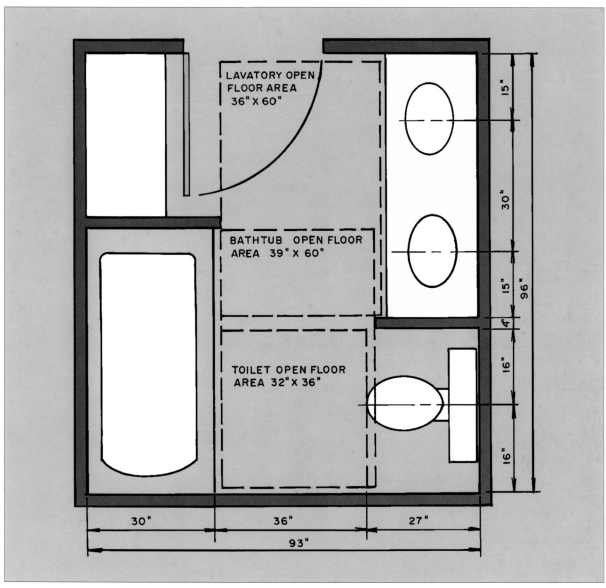

LAVATORY OPEN
FLOOR AREA
36" X 60"

BATHTUB OPEN FLOOR
AREA 39" X 60"

TOILET OPEN FLOOR
AREA 32" X 36"

15"

30"

15"

4"

16"

16"

96"

30"

36"

27"

93"

5-12 Layout for full bath. Double lavatories and a storage cabinet increase the usefulness of the bathroom. Allow more open area, whenever possible.

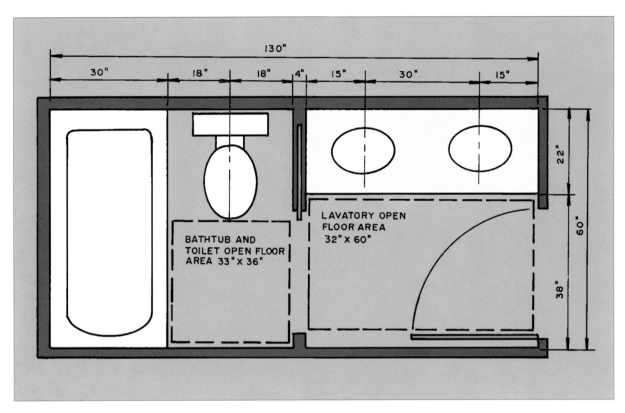

130"

30" 18" 18" 4" 15" 30" 15"

22"

60"

38"

BATHTUB AND
TOILET OPEN FLOOR
AREA 33" x 36"

LAVATORY OPEN
FLOOR AREA
32" x 60"

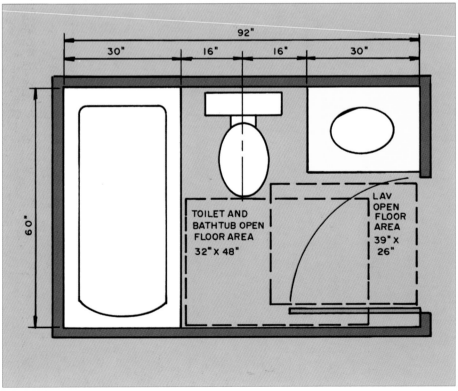

92"

30" 16" 16" 30"

60"

TOILET AND
BATHTUB OPEN
FLOOR AREA
32" x 48"

LAV
OPEN
FLOOR
AREA
39" x
26"

5-13 Layouts for full
baths with minimum
open floor area
allowances. At top, the
bathtub and toilet are
in a compartment,
and the open floor
areas are minimal.
To the left is a tight
plan. The bathtub is
crowded but usable,
and the lavatory aisle
is a bit narrow. Allow
more open area,
whenever possible.

CONSTRUCTING BATHROOMS

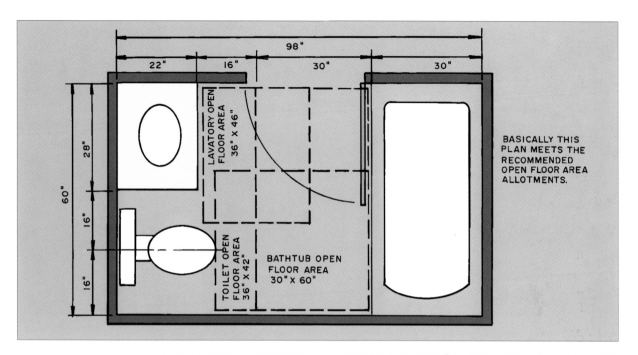

98"

22"   16"   30"   30"

60"   28"

16"

16"

LAVATORY OPEN FLOOR AREA 36" X 46"

TOILET OPEN FLOOR AREA 36" X 42"

BATHTUB OPEN FLOOR AREA 30" X 60"

BASICALLY THIS PLAN MEETS THE RECOMMENDED OPEN FLOOR AREA ALLOTMENTS.

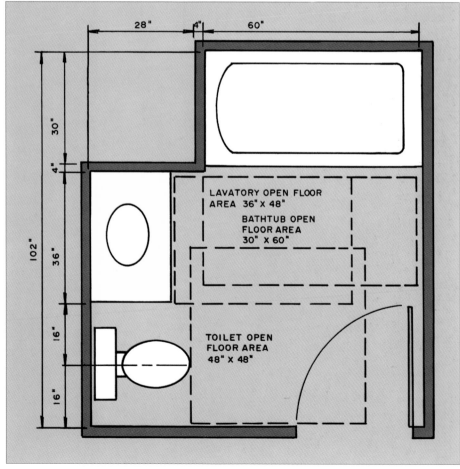

28"   4"   60"

30"

4"

102"   36"

16"

16"

LAVATORY OPEN FLOOR AREA 36" X 48"

BATHTUB OPEN FLOOR AREA 30" X 60"

TOILET OPEN FLOOR AREA 48" X 48"

5-14 Alternative layouts for full bath. Both these plans have the recommended open floor area for each fixture. Allow more open area, whenever possible.

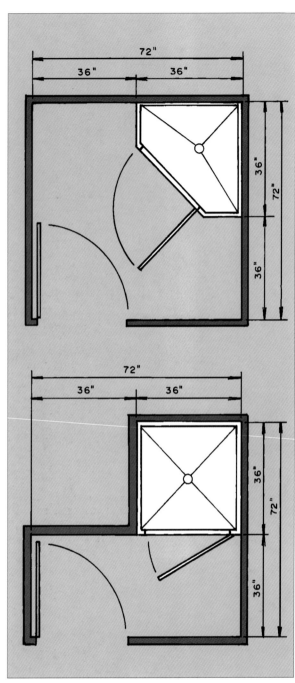

5-15 A small shower room provides
a second bathing facility at little cost.

If space is really tight and you want to add more bathing facilities, consider adding a shower room. This will double your bathing capacities and is a lot less expensive than adding a full bathroom. Observe the space planning requirements and be certain to include a ceiling ventilating fan (5-15). One interesting technique is to use a corner stall, opening up a little more floor area.

LARGER, SPACIOUS LAYOUTS

Minimum bathroom layouts are not recommended except for situations where space or money is limited. For a little additional cost the allocation of additional floor space makes the bathroom easier and more pleasant to use. When space and cost are not major factors the arrangements for a larger, luxurious bathroom have almost unlimited possibilities. One step beyond the three fixture full bathroom is to add a separate shower as shown in 5-16. This shower is safer and easier to use than a shower in a bathtub and is very helpful for children and those with physical limitations who have difficulty getting into the bathtub.

A really luxurious bath will have a whirlpool, toilet in a private compartment, two lavatories, a bidet, a bathtub and a shower, a dressing area, and a vanity for grooming. Examples of attractive whirlpools are shown in 5-17 and 5-18. The layouts possible are many but a couple are shown in 5-19 through 5-22, on the following pages.

5-16 This is a nice master bathroom. It has both a double lavatory, a shower and a bathtub, and has open floor area greater than the minimum recommendations.

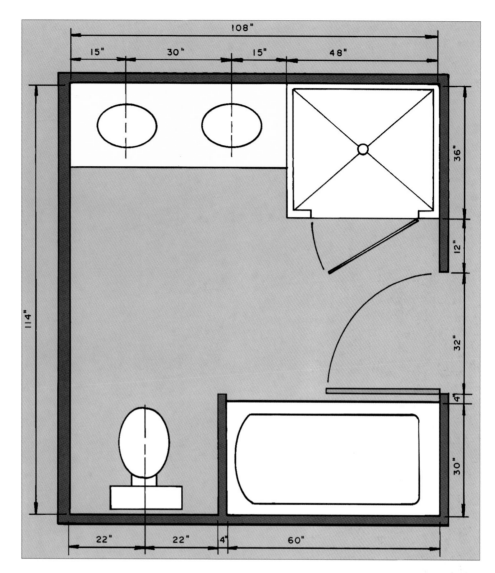

5-17 This raised whirlpool located beside a window is a cheerful place to relax.

5-18 A corner-mounted whirlpool or bathtub provides an attractive feature to the bathroom. Notice the platform has a ceramic tile finish material.

DESIGNING THE BATHROOM LAYOUT

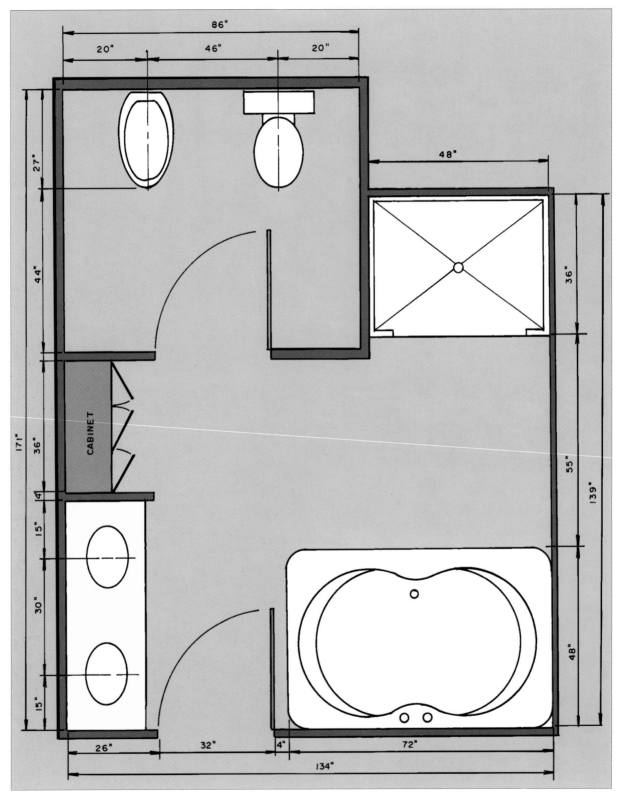

5-19 This spacious bathroom provides multiple fixtures and a degree of privacy.

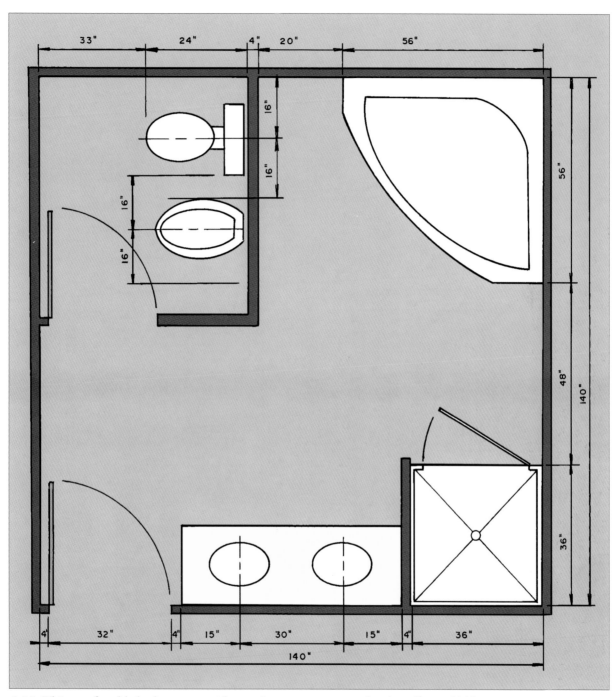

5-20 This comfortable bathroom provides a private compartment for the toilet and bidet
plus a corner-mounted whirlpool.

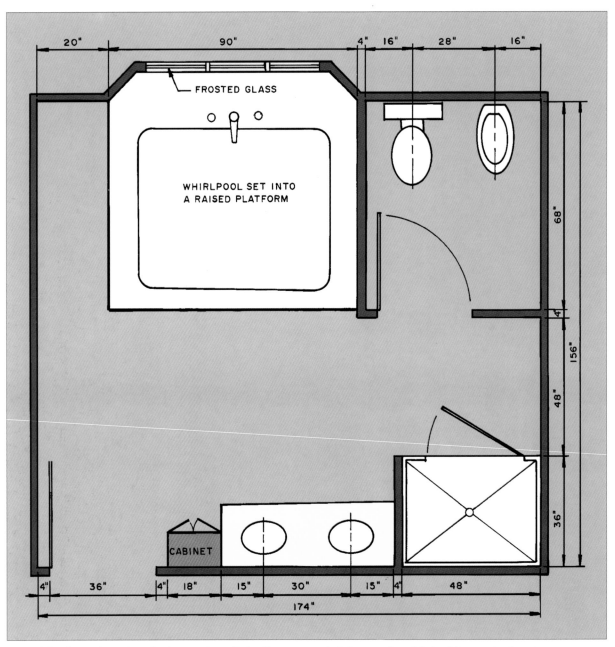

FROSTED GLASS

WHIRLPOOL SET INTO
A RAISED PLATFORM

CABINET

5-21 This large, luxurious bathroom has all the fixtures needed for comfortable bathing and relaxation.

CONSTRUCTING BATHROOMS

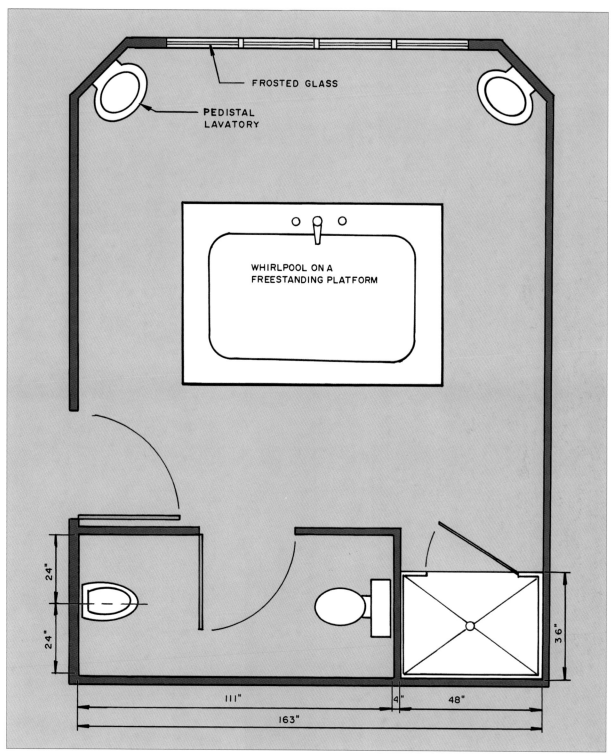

FROSTED GLASS

PEDISTAL
LAVATORY

WHIRLPOOL ON A
FREESTANDING PLATFORM

24"

24"

36"

111"

4"

48"

163"

5-22 This large, luxurious bathroom has a freestanding whirlpool on a raised platform. This is the striking feature you notice as you enter the room. Notice the use of two pedestal lavatories.

CHAPTER 6

Electrical, Lighting & Plumbing

Courtesy Wellborn Cabinet, Inc.

The electrical requirements for the typical bathroom are not large unless fixtures requiring considerable current, such as an electric heater, whirlpool, or a sauna, are included. The lights, electric outlets, and ventilating fans require 120 volt current (**6-1**). The electrician can calculate what each requires and specify the number of circuits needed. Some fixtures require so much current or 240V that they should be on a separate circuit. Among these are:

Whirlpools
Saunas
Electric water heaters for a spa
Infrared heaters
Heater-light-ventilation units
Electric wall heaters

If you are remodeling an older house the power delivered at the service panel may be as small as 60A (amperes). You may have to upgrade your electrical service to handle some of these fixtures. Check your local building code for specific requirements.

6-1 The lavatory in this base cabinet receives additional illumination from the series of frosted lights (illuminaries) above the mirror.

AMPERES, VOLTS & WATTS

An **ampere** is a unit of the **rate of flow** of electric current. This is in general similar to the number of gallons of water that will flow through a pipe. The electric current is under **pressure,** similar to water in a pipe being under pressure. The unit of **electrical pressure** is the **volt.** The **amount of power** in a circuit is given in **watts.** A watt is the result of volts × amperes (flow × pressure).

ELECTRICAL RECEPTACLE OUTLETS

Typically codes require one receptacle outlet on the wall by the lavatory (**6-2**). Under no conditions should these receptacle outlets be installed faceup on the lavatory countertop. The lavatory outlets typically are used for small appliances such as an electric toothbrush, hair dryer, or shaver. They are typically 20A (ampere) circuits and one circuit for these is often specified. Additional receptacle outlets in the walls are used for such items as a vacuum cleaner. In a small bathroom one outlet on a convenient wall is enough. Larger bathrooms may have several, but do not space more than 10 or 12 feet apart. All receptacle outlets in the bathroom must be on a ground-fault circuit interrupter (GFCI).

There are other requirements specified in the National Electrical Code that must be observed by the electrician as circuits are designed. The number of receptacles allowed by code permits more of them to be on a general-purpose circuit than on an appliance circuit.

GROUND-FAULT CIRCUIT INTERRUPTERS

A ground-fault circuit interrupter (GFCI) is a device that monitors the amount of current going to a load (such as a hair dryer) and compares it with the amount leaving the appliance. If the two amounts are equal, the electricity is flowing properly. However, if some of the electrons are missing on the flow away from the appliance, the current leaving is less than that going into it. Therefore there is a leakage in the system. The GFCI detects this difference and opens the circuit. This leakage is too small to trip a circuit breaker or blow a fuse, yet current is leaking from the circuit. This could be running through the person using the appliance to a ground; it is actually a short in the circuit. The GFCI will open the circuit in ⅟30 of a second, keeping you from getting a bad shock. The imbalance of current flow that the GFCI detects is four to six milliamps (thousandths of an ampere). This means you might get a shock but it will only last for ⅟30 of a second. Most people can withstand this shock before their heart goes into fibrillation. Fibrillation is when the heart goes out of sync, resulting in death.

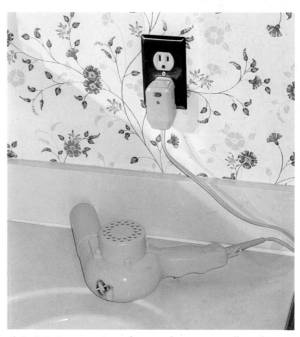

6-2 It is important to have at least one wall outlet by the lavatory

GFCI TYPES

For your residence you can have a circuit-breaker GFCI or use a receptacle GFCI. The **circuit-breaker GFCI** is mounted in the service entrance panel and provides protection on all receptacles on that circuit. The **receptacle GFCI** is placed in the outlet box instead of a standard convenience outlet. It protects only those things plugged into that one receptacle. It looks like a standard receptacle but has a test and reset button. If the appliance plugged into it trips it, you can unplug the appliance and restore power to the receptacle by pressing the reset button (**6-3**). The receptacle can be tested by pressing the test button and reset by pressing the reset button.

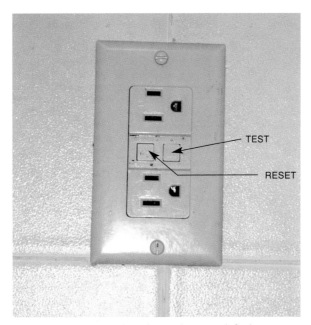

TEST

RESET

6-3 A wall-mounted outlet with ground-fault circuit interruption protection.

Building codes specify where GFCI protection must be installed, and the bathroom is one place it should be used. Codes require all receptacles within a 6-foot straight-line distance from a sink to have GFCI protection. Check your local code to verify the requirements.

BATHROOM LIGHTING

As you plan the lighting, you will need some type of **general lighting** for the room. You will also need **task lighting** that focuses on a limited area, such as at a lavatory. If you wish you could add some **special lighting** to illuminate some architectural feature such as a cathedral ceiling.

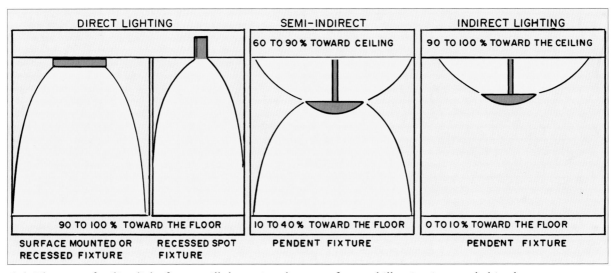

DIRECT LIGHTING		SEMI–INDIRECT	INDIRECT LIGHTING
		60 TO 90 % TOWARD CEILING	90 TO 100 % TOWARD THE CEILING
90 TO 100 % TOWARD THE FLOOR		10 TO 40 % TOWARD THE FLOOR	0 TO 10 % TOWARD THE FLOOR
SURFACE MOUNTED OR RECESSED FIXTURE	RECESSED SPOT FIXTURE	PENDENT FIXTURE	PENDENT FIXTURE

6-4 The type of ceiling light fixture will determine the type of general illumination needed in the room.

6-5 This decorative bathroom ceiling light also has a ventilating fan behind the light, pulling in air in the grill around the edges.

6-6 Recessed light fixtures can be located around the ceiling to provide general illumination in an area such as a shower.

GENERAL LIGHTING

Since most bathrooms are rather small, a single light near the center of the room will provide adequate general lighting. This is often a part of a ventilation unit that contains a fan and the light (6-5). If the bathroom is larger you may want two or more ceiling lights. Small recessed ceiling mounted fixtures (6-6) can be spaced around the ceiling to provide general illumination. They use either spot or flood bulbs. In general you want a low-wattage bulb because high intensity illumination is not required or even desired in a bathroom.

Also used are surface-mounted incandescent fixtures as shown in 6-7. These are available in a wide variety of designs and can have one to three incandescent bulbs. Again use low-wattage bulbs because the illumination usually desired is even but not intense.

The type of fixture and its placement will control how much light is directed to the ceiling and how much is directed to the floor (6-4). **Direct light** projects most of the light to the floor. It produces considerable glare. **Indirect** and **semi-indirect** illuminaries have an opaque reflector that directs most of the light to the ceiling, relying on reflected light to illuminate the room. This produces less glare than the direct illuminaries.

6-7 Various ceiling-mounted incandescent lighting fixtures provide good, widespread general illumination.

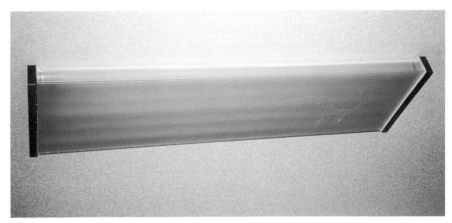

6-9 A typical dimmer switch. Press it in to turn the light on and off. Rotate it to change the intensity of the light.

6-8 This surface-mounted fluorescent fixture will provide broad general illumination. Recessed fixtures are also available.

Surface-mounted and recessed fluorescent fixtures are also used, especially in larger bathrooms (6-8).You will need to provide illumination in compartments in which a fixture such as a toilet or shower is located. Recessed spot fixtures are commonly used (6-6 and 6-13). They can be controlled by a switch separate from the overall general illumination circuit if you wish.

Consider the use of a dimmer switch on all types of lighting. It will let you vary the intensity by simply turning the knob. Press in on the knob to shut off the light (6-9). Different dimmer switches are needed for incandescent and fluorescent lights, so be certain to check this as you buy one.

6-10 A series of shaded wall-hung incandescent lamps placed above the mirror at the lavatory provide excellent illumination.

CONSTRUCTING BATHROOMS

TASK LIGHTING

Task lighting is used at the lavatory sink so you can see clearly in the mirror as you shave, brush teeth, or work on your hair. Typically it involves illuminaries above the mirror (**6-10** and refer to **6-1**). Another place these are required is if you have a vanity for grooming and makeup. Recessed tube lights are often set in the ceiling above the lavatory to provide additional local illumination (**6-11**).

You can vary the illumination by the wattage of the bulbs you install and can use bulbs often referred to as "soft light" if they give you the results you want.

6-11 Notice the two recessed tube lights in the ceiling above this lavatory. The dark wood and wall covering make additional illumination very important.

Courtesy Aristokraft, Inc.

SPECIAL LIGHTING

Special lighting is used to enhance the overall appearance of the room or illuminate a particular architectural feature. It could be some form of 120V illuminairie or a low-voltage system.

A small track light system could be used to illuminate a special feature (**6-12**). The lights are adjustable, giving a wide range of illumination. Another illuminairie is a recessed fixture with a revolving socket often called the eyeball (**6-13**). It can be used to focus light on a wall or painting.

LIGHTING CONTROLS

The most commonly used switch is a single-pole single-throw switch. This type of switch operates one light or a series of connected lights from one location. Often it is desirable to be able to operate some of the lights, especially those used for general illumination, from two different locations. To do this, use a three-way switch. It will turn the light on and off from two locations. A light can be controlled from three locations by using two three-way switches and one four-way switch.

The effectiveness of lighting can be enhanced by using a dimmer switch. The intensity of the light produced can be varied from off to full brightness by sliding or turning the dimmer switch knob (refer to **6-8**). Different dimmer switches are required for incandescent and fluorescent fixtures.

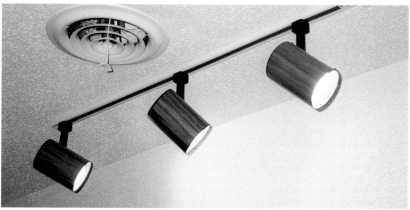

6-12 Track lighting provides a very flexible means of lighting special features. Each light can be moved along the length of the track and the angle of projection changed.

6-13 This recessed incandescent fixture permits the light to be rotated so it can illuminate a special feature in the bathroom. It is sometimes referred to as an eyeball fixture.

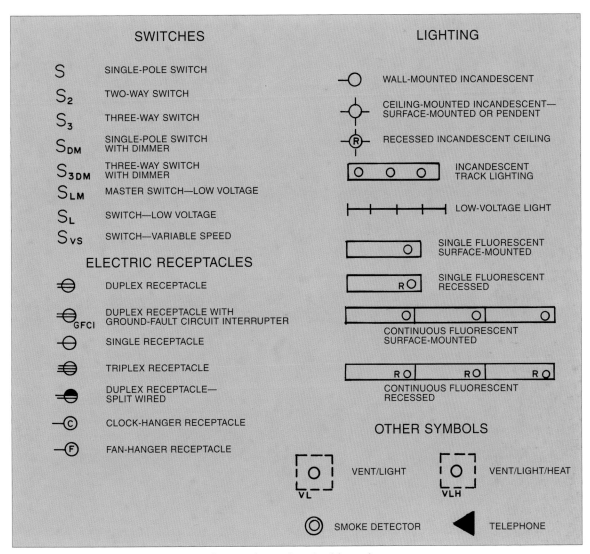

SWITCHES

S — SINGLE-POLE SWITCH

S_2 — TWO-WAY SWITCH

S_3 — THREE-WAY SWITCH

S_{DM} — SINGLE-POLE SWITCH WITH DIMMER

S_{3DM} — THREE-WAY SWITCH WITH DIMMER

S_{LM} — MASTER SWITCH—LOW VOLTAGE

S_L — SWITCH—LOW VOLTAGE

S_{VS} — SWITCH—VARIABLE SPEED

ELECTRIC RECEPTACLES

DUPLEX RECEPTACLE

DUPLEX RECEPTACLE WITH GROUND-FAULT CIRCUIT INTERRUPTER

SINGLE RECEPTACLE

TRIPLEX RECEPTACLE

DUPLEX RECEPTACLE— SPLIT WIRED

CLOCK-HANGER RECEPTACLE

FAN-HANGER RECEPTACLE

LIGHTING

WALL-MOUNTED INCANDESCENT

CEILING-MOUNTED INCANDESCENT— SURFACE-MOUNTED OR PENDENT

RECESSED INCANDESCENT CEILING

INCANDESCENT TRACK LIGHTING

LOW-VOLTAGE LIGHT

SINGLE FLUORESCENT SURFACE-MOUNTED

SINGLE FLUORESCENT RECESSED

CONTINUOUS FLUORESCENT SURFACE-MOUNTED

CONTINUOUS FLUORESCENT RECESSED

OTHER SYMBOLS

VENT/LIGHT

VENT/LIGHT/HEAT

SMOKE DETECTOR

TELEPHONE

6-14 Some of the electrical symbols frequently used on building plans.

DRAWING THE ELECTRICAL & LIGHTING PLAN

Typically the floor plan used for the electrical and lighting plan is a copy of the detailed plan showing the layout. Some architects and designers prefer to show dimensions giving room size and locating the fixtures. Others will locate the symbols on the drawing. You may want to show plumbing, heating, air conditioning, and ventilation systems on the same plan. Some of the electrical symbols frequently used on building plans are shown in **6-14.**

A typical electrical and lighting plan is shown in **6-15**. Refer to **6-14** for identification of the electrical symbols. The specifications detailing the brand, specific type, and other details identifying each light fixture are listed separately on a light fixture schedule. This plan locates the lights by dimensions from the walls of the room and between fixtures. It shows all the required receptacles and other electrical connections. The lights are connected to switches with a curved line and a curved line also connects all lights controlled by one switch.

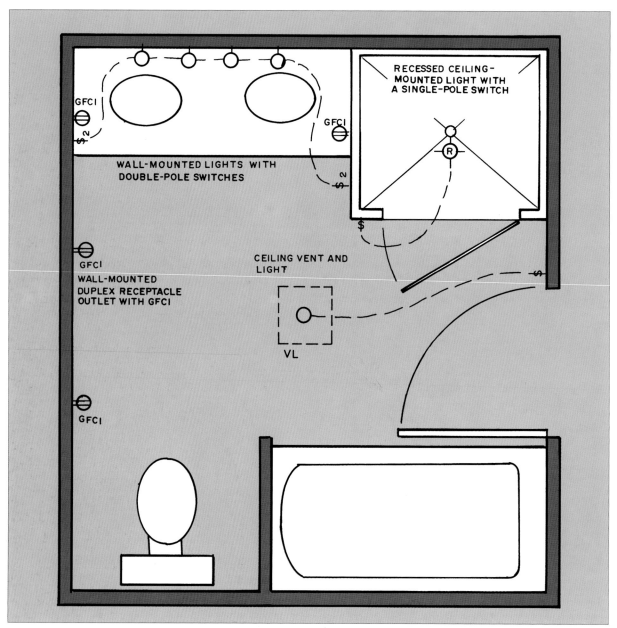

6-15 A typical electrical plan for a small bathroom. Sometimes the location of each item is dimensioned on the drawing. Refer to 6-14 for the meaning of the electrical symbols.

PLUMBING

The plumbing system involves bringing potable hot and cold water to the fixtures and removing all waste water and materials. The walls and floors around plumbing fixtures must be of a finish that is easily cleaned and water resistant.

The water is delivered to the fixtures under pressure from a public water utility or a private well. The waste is discharged by gravity to a public utility waste disposal system or a private septic tank. In some cases it must be removed by a pump raising it up to the level of the city sewer line.

If you are remodeling an old bathroom you might find the water lines are partially clogged or have deteriorated to the point where they cannot carry the flow needed by the new fixtures and may actually rupture and fail due to age. The first thing to do is to see if anything needs to be replaced.

If the new fixture location requires moving the pipes it is logical to replace them. Trying to move old plumbing is not a good idea. Likewise, the waste pipes face the same problems as old water pipes and possibly can be in even worse condition.

New water pipes will be typically ¾-inch diameter and have to operate under 50 to 60 pounds of pressure. Copper and plastic pipe are widely used. Copper is used for both hot and cold water. You need to be careful when choosing plastic pipe. Polyvinyl chloride (PVC) is used for **cold water** lines and drain, waste, and vent (DWV) pipes. Chlorinated polyvinyl chloride (CPVC) is used for **hot** and **cold water** lines. Acrylonitrile-butadiene-styrene (ABS) is used for drain, waste, and vent piping. Check your codes for permissible pipe materials.

In older houses you will find galvanized steel water pipe. It is seldom used in new construction. It is difficult to install because it is rigid and requires threaded fittings. Plastic pipe can be connected to it with special fittings. Copper pipe may also be connected to it but you must use dielectric (nonconducting) fittings. If these are not used, a small current flow is created due to galvanic action and causing corrosion and eventual leaks.

A plan for a waste removal system is shown in **6-16**. Each fixture is connected to a vertical soil stack with waste lines. The pictorial illus-

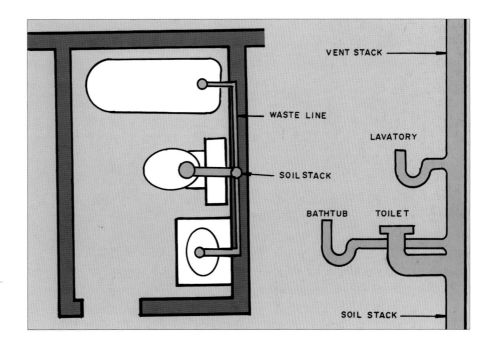

6-16 A plan for a waste disposal system for a small bathroom.

tration in **6-17** shows these connections. The soil stack carries the waste to the house drain, which carries it outside the house and connects to the house sewer.

Be certain that the waste removal system is vented. The venting of such a system is shown in **6-17**. The fixture vent lines connect to the vent stack extending out of the roof of the house. The vent lines are dry lines and connect to the verti-

cal vent stack well above the waste line connections. The vents release sewer gases into the vent stack, which then releases them to the atmosphere. The vents keep the system operating at atmospheric pressure. If a fixture, such as a lavatory, is not vented the flow of liquid waste could pull the water out of the trap. This would let sewer gas into the room through the lavatory drain (**6-18**).

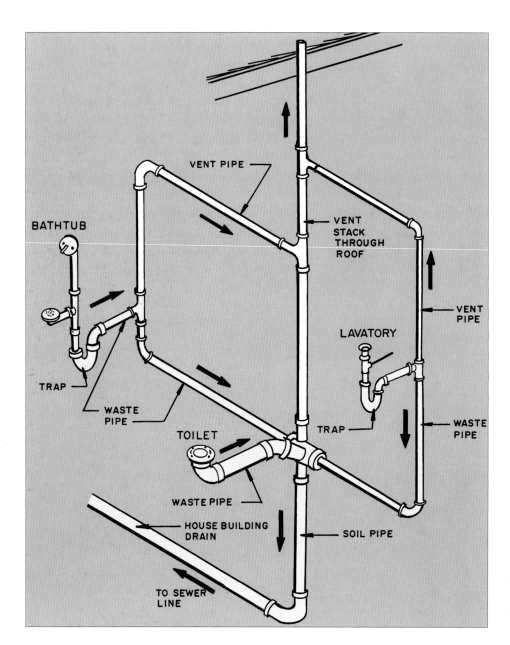

6-17 Typical piping for a waste disposal system for a small bathroom. Details can vary depending upon the fixtures and local plumbing codes.

CONSTRUCTING BATHROOMS

Each fixture will have a trap. Most likely you will find a P-trap that is code approved. The S-trap will be found in older homes and is no longer approved. When the water leaves the lavatory, atmospheric pressure tends to force the water in the trap down the pipe, leaving the amount of water in the S-trap inadequate to seal off the gases (6-19). Lavatories, bathtubs, and

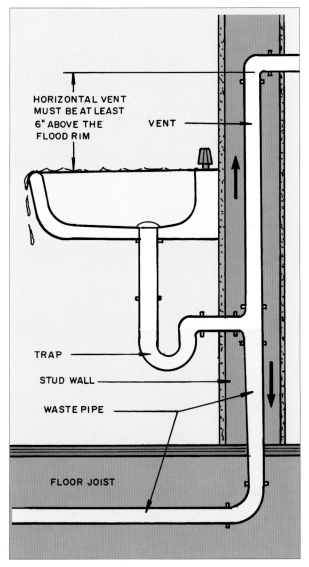

6-18 The trap stays filled with water preventing sewer gas from entering the room through the lavatory or bathtub drain.

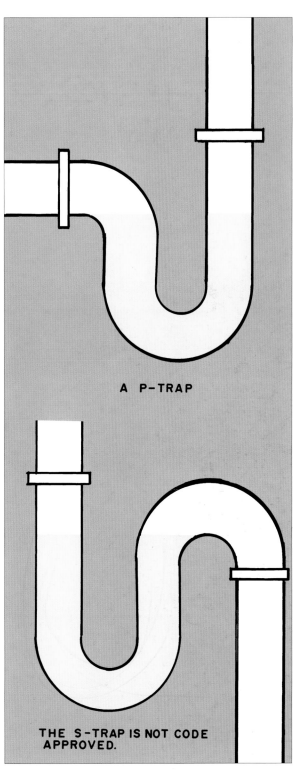

6-19 P-traps are code approved for lavatories and bathtubs. The S-trap is no longer approved and should be replaced if you find one in your house.

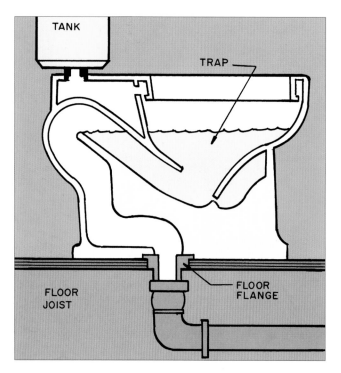

showers use a P-trap. You may find a drum trap in some old installations. The toilet bowl serves as a trap as shown in **6-20**.

POTABLE WATER SYSTEMS

When the water is shut off quickly in a potable water system, there are water hammer mufflers that absorb the shock. Old systems simply had air capped in a pipe, but modern systems have a bladder that absorbs the shock, eliminating the annoying hammering noise (**6-21**).

6-20 The water remaining in the toilet bowl forms a trap blocking sewer gases from entering the bathroom.

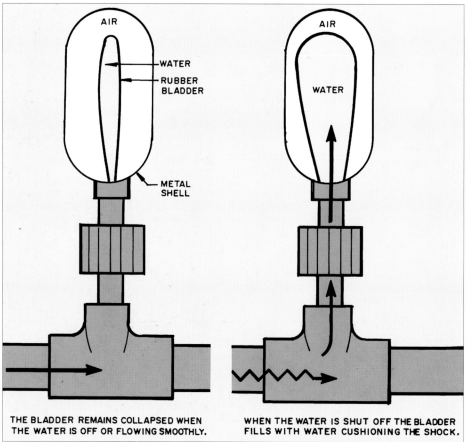

THE BLADDER REMAINS COLLAPSED WHEN THE WATER IS OFF OR FLOWING SMOOTHLY.

WHEN THE WATER IS SHUT OFF THE BLADDER FILLS WITH WATER CUSHIONING THE SHOCK.

6-21 Water hammering that occurs when the water is shut off quickly can be eliminated by using a water hammer muffler.

CONSTRUCTING BATHROOMS

A typical potable water system to a bathroom is shown in **6-22**. Notice the water hammer mufflers that are on the hot and the cold water lines. This water hammer muffler chamber has pressurized air surrounding a bladder filled with water linked to both the water system lines.

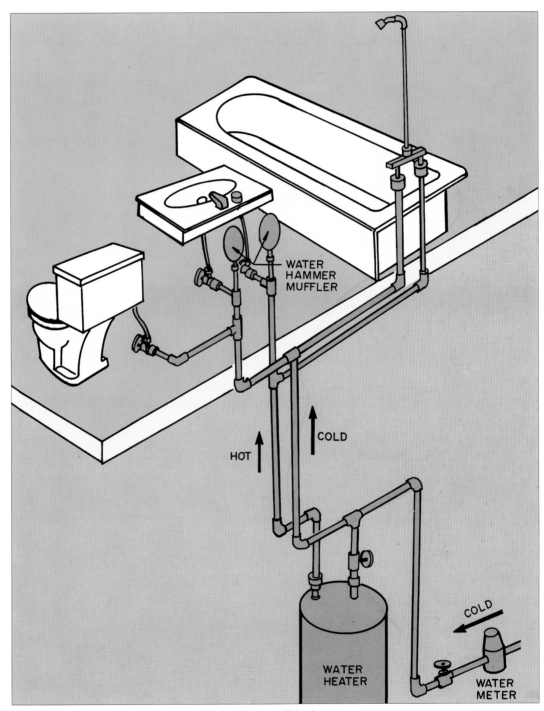

6-22 A typical hot and cold water system to a small bathroom.

BATHROOM VENTILATION

Plumbing codes specify that a bathroom must have a window that can be opened or some form of mechanical ventilation. Actually even if you have a window, it is a good idea to put in an exhaust fan, because the window is seldom opened. The fan running for around 30 minutes during a shower will carry the air with high moisture content out of the room and return the moisture content to normal. If you do not remove moisture, windows will sweat and mildew will form on interior surfaces, causing a smell and the paint and wallpaper to deteriorate. Hopefully the exterior wall has a vapor barrier to keep the moisture from entering it and damaging the insulation, studs, sheathing, and exterior siding.

6-24 This ceiling-mounted ventilation fan also has a light in the center providing general illumination in the bathroom.

6-23 This ceiling ventilation fan removes humid air from the bathroom and discharges it outside the house.

6-25 This beautiful ceiling light provides general illumination and contains a ventilating fan that pulls air in through the grill openings next to the ceiling.

6-26 This ceiling ventilating unit also has infrared radiant heat lamps to give you rapid heat after your shower.

Check your local code for ventilation requirements. Typically they require a window to provide 1.5 square feet of open area.

MECHANICAL VENTILATION

Ventilating fans are usually located in the ceiling near the center of the bathroom. Some types have only a fan (**6-23**) while others have a light (**6-24** and **6-25**) for general illumination and a fan. These are wired so the fan comes on when you turn on the light. However, you can wire each to separate switches if you wish more control over when the fan runs.

Another type has a fan and infrared heat lamps providing rapid radiant heat (**6-26**). In **6-27** is a unit containing a ventilation fan, light fixture, and an electric space heater. There are bathroom vent fans that have automatic humidity and motion sensors and a night light. Some use compact energy-efficient fluorescent bulbs that will last many years. The humidity sensor starts the fan when it senses excess moisture in the air and shuts it off when the moisture level returns to normal. The motion sensor notices when you leave the bathroom and forget to turn off the light. It shuts it off. The night light has a 7-watt bulb providing enough light for bathroom use at night (**6-28**).

6-27 This ceiling unit contains a ventilating fan, light, and electric space heater.

6-28 This unit has a ventilating fan, light, electric heater plus a night light.

Remember, a ventilating fan cannot remove the volume of air it is designed to move if the bathroom is tightly closed. One way to increase air flow into the bathroom is to leave a ½ to ¾ inch space at the bottom of the door. Running with the door open a crack is even better.

Consider the noise produced by the fan. Some are very noisy, especially in a small room, and can be heard all over the house. Select a fan that has a low sone rating. A **sone** is a unit of loudness. Try to get a fan that is rated at 2 sones or less.

You must calculate the volume of the room in cubic feet to determine the size of fan you need. Fans are rated by the number of cubic feet per minute (ft^3/m) they can move. It is recommended that a fan should be able to change the air in a room eight times per hour.

To find the fan required, multiply the width × length × height (**6-29**) to get the total cubic feet (cf). Multiply this by 8 changes per hour and divide by 60 minutes to get the cubic feet per minute (cf/m) that the fan must move.

Bathroom 8 × 8× 10 ft = 640 cf
640 cf × 8 changes per hour = 5120 cf/h
5120 cf/h ÷ 60 minutes/h
= 85 cf/m fan capacity

Use ducts that are hard and smooth inside. Avoid turns because this slows down the air and reduces the amount of the flow.

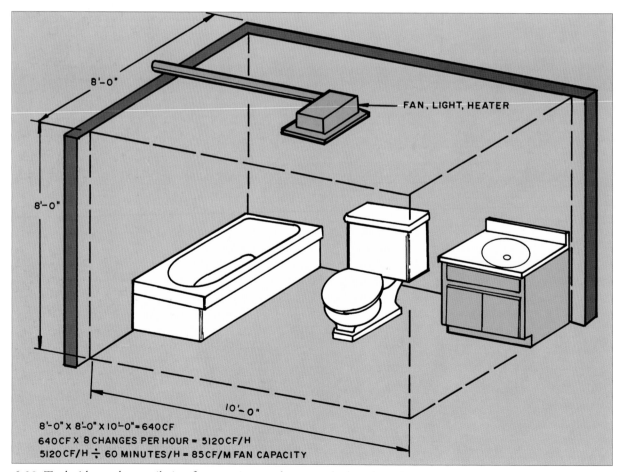

6-29 To decide on the ventilating fan capacity, you have to calculate the volume of the bathroom in cubic feet (cf).

CONSTRUCTING BATHROOMS

6-30 This infrared heat lamp unit can be placed wherever you want spot heat, such as over the area directly outside the shower.

SHORT-TERM HEAT

When you bathe, you generally like the air temperature a bit higher than normal. This can be provided with infrared heat lamps (**6-30**) or electric heaters in the ventilating fan as shown in **6-27** and **6-28**. Considerably more heat can be provided with a wall-mounted electric heater (**6-31**) or an electric baseboard heater (**6-32**).

The infrared heat lamp has the advantage that it does not heat the air but heats anything that its

6-31 An electric wall heater provides considerable heat very rapidly and heats the entire room.

rays strike. This gives you instant heat. The electric resistance heater must heat all the air in the room to get the temperature up, but you can stand near it and get some rapid heat.

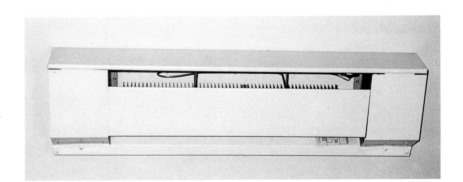

6-32 This is a small electric baseboard heater. It is available in various lengths and wattages.

CHAPTER 7

Bathroom Floors, Walls & Ceilings

The floor, walls, and ceiling provide the finished appearance of your bathroom. There are a number of things to consider as you make decisions on how to finish each of these.

Keep in mind the **cost**. As you choose materials, keep a record of the cost of those you prefer. Consider the **permanence** of the material. For example, carpet on the floor can be easily changed but a ceramic tile floor is more permanent. Then consider how the materials resist **water**, **humidity**, **mold**, and **mildew**. Some are quite water resistant, and mold and mildew are easily washed away. Others are susceptible to eventual damage. The **texture** of the material produces various reactions. A hard material, such as a ceramic tile floor, produces a cool, clean feeling whereas a soft resilient material, such as a

Courtesy American Standard, Inc.

7-1 The warm colors on the walls and floor provide a subdued, restful atmosphere. The warm, wood-framed doors and door casing and baseboard add to the overall atmosphere. The wood-framed whirlpool stands cleanly in contrast to the overall elements.

carpet, produces a luxurious sensation. The texture can also influence the ease of cleaning. A heavily textured surface, such as a woven fiber material, is much harder to clean than a smooth surface, such as painted gypsum drywall.

A major consideration is the use of **color**. Color can, for very little expense, add more to the interior than any other element. It sets the atmosphere. Warm colors, such as yellow, orange, brown, and red, make the room seem cheery and restful (**7-1**) while cool colors, such as green, blue, and white provide a feeling of lightness and freshness (**7-2**). Color is provided by fixtures, cabinets, and accessories but the major impact is from the large areas of the floor, walls, and ceiling. Remember, darker hues tend

7-2 The cool blue walls—enhanced by the white pedestal lavatory, window, massive baseboard, and painted wood floors—presents a clean, light, refreshing atmosphere.

Courtesy American Standard, Inc.

to absorb light while lighter hues reflect light. Dark surfaces look foreshortened while light colors visually extend a surface (7-3). For example, a dark ceiling will appear lower. Narrow, tight spaces can appear larger by using light-colored walls, ceiling, and floor (7-4).

As you view the overall selection of materials, their texture, and color, try to visualize how they will look when assembled into the finished bathroom. The color of the fixtures should be in harmony with the wall, ceiling, and flooring materials (7-5).

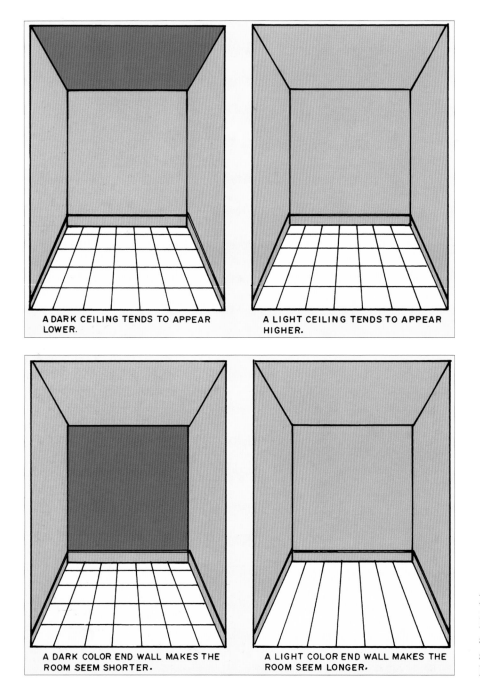

A DARK CEILING TENDS TO APPEAR LOWER.

A LIGHT CEILING TENDS TO APPEAR HIGHER.

A DARK COLOR END WALL MAKES THE ROOM SEEM SHORTER.

A LIGHT COLOR END WALL MAKES THE ROOM SEEM LONGER.

7-3 The use of dark and light colors can make a room seem larger or smaller and the ceiling higher or lower.

CONSTRUCTING BATHROOMS

Finally, if you plan to install the floor, wall, and ceiling finish materials, understand what it takes to do the job. Installing ceramic tile on walls is a lot harder than painting them or installing wallpaper.

FLOOR COVERING MATERIALS

The commonly used bathroom floor-covering materials range from carpet, providing a soft, luxurious feeling, to hard, clean ceramic tile. Each material has advantages and disadvantages. For example, carpet when frequently wet is slow to dry and will develop mold. A glossy glazed ceramic tile, while tough and water resistant, can be slippery. As you make your choice consider the range of products available and carefully consider their features. Ideally you want something that is resistant to moisture, not slippery, and can be cleaned with ordinary household cleaners.

Courtesy Kohler Company

7-4 This long, narrow, corridor-type bathroom is made to appear larger and less confining by keeping the fixtures, floor, walls, and cabinets a light color.

7-5 The white fixtures and cabinets are in harmony. The cabinets are trimmed in a natural hardwood that blends with the slightly darker wall color. The light-color floor ties it all together and a bit of color is added by the area rug.

Courtesy Aristokraft, Inc.

CERAMIC FLOOR TILE

Not all ceramic tile can be used on floors. That designed for walls will not perform adequately on floors. Ceramic floor tiles are water resistant but must be installed with a grout between them that is also water resistant.

Select floor tiles that have a rough-textured matt surface rather than a glossy glazed finish. The matt finish tends to be slip resistant while glossy tiles are very slippery. Consider laying a area rug in the center of the room, as seen in 7-5. It should have a rubberized slip-resistant backing. It can soften the floor a bit and serve as a bath mat. When wet it should be hung to dry.

Ceramic floor tiles are available in 4-, 6-, 8-, 12-, and 16-inch squares. They are typically 5/16 inch thick and laid with 1/4 inch space for grout (7-6). They are available in a wide range of colors, patterns, and textures.

Porcelain stone tiles are made from refined ceramic materials and porcelain and are high quality. They are available in the same sizes as ceramic floor tile. They are as strong as stone and the color goes through the thickness of the tile.

Quarry tiles are available glazed or unglazed. They range in color from red to brown to buff. They are usually 1/2 to 3/4 inch thick and in squares, rectangles, and other shapes. The color runs through the thickness. The unglazed are slip-resistant.

Paver tiles are made from natural clays and are much like quarry tile. They are usually a bit thinner, ranging from 3/8 to 1/2 inch. Unglazed types are slip-resistant.

Courtesy American Olean Tile Company

7-6 This beautiful bathroom has a ceramic tile floor with ceramic wall covering, door-opening framing, and carved ceramic accents. It frames the whirlpool and a shelf below the window. The entire room is in a balanced harmony.

INSTALLING CERAMIC FLOOR TILE

The various types of ceramic floor tiles are bonded to a 3/4-inch thick underlayment-grade plywood subfloor with mastic. However, it is highly recommended that you bond a 1/4-inch cement board over the plywood with mastic and bond the tile to it. This produces a water-resistant layer below the tile and the tile sticks to it better (7-7). To install the cement backer board trowel a layer of mastic over the subfloor and place the backer board in it. Then mechanically secure it to the subfloor with backer board screws or galvanized roofing nails. Space these 8 inches apart on the edges of the panels and on 16-inch O.C. rows in the field of the panel. Fill the joints between the panels with the mastic and cover them with a fiberglass mesh tape. This keeps any moisture that may have penetrated the grout from getting to the wood subfloor.

CARPET

While carpets are not widely used in bathrooms, they can be effectively used in areas such as a dressing area, where moisture from bathing or damp areas as around the toilet does not reach (refer to 7-1). The problem with carpet is that after it gets repeated wettings it will hold the moisture and mold will develop. If installed directly on the plywood subfloor the moisture will cause it to deteriorate, making it necessary to replace the plywood. However, properly selected carpet if kept clean and if dried after use will last for years before it needs to be replaced. Good ventilation in the bathroom will extend the life of the carpet. It helps to choose a carpet with a short nap.

Carpet can be installed over any smooth subfloor. It can be laid over a carpet pad and secured with tackless strips around the wall (7-8) or bonded directly to the subfloor with a mastic.

When choosing a carpet seek the advice of the dealer. Some materials are more suitable than others for exposure to moisture.

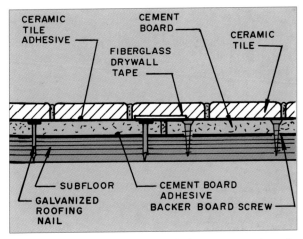

7-7 Ceramic floor tile are bonded to a cement board underlayment with a mastic. The cement board is bonded and screwed to the subfloor.

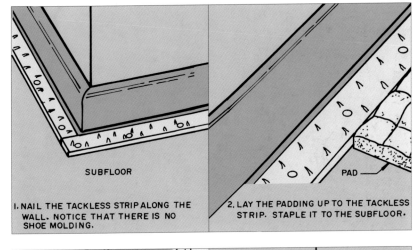

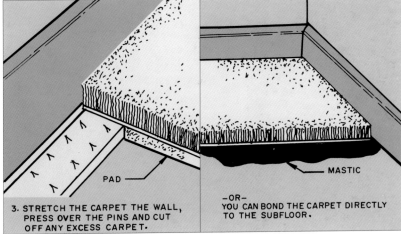

7-8 Carpet is laid on tackless strips or bonded with mastic to the subfloor.

Carpets are available made from **natural fiber** and a variety of **synthetic fibers**. Some carpets are made with a blend of natural and synthetic fibers, so discuss the merits of each with your carpet dealer. Wool is a natural fiber. Synthetic fibers include polypropylene (olefin), polyester, nylon, modacrylic, and acrylic.

Wool is a fiber obtained from sheep. It has good resistance to abrasion and aging and resists damage from sunlight and mildew.

Polypropylene is a class of olefin containing 85 percent propylene by weight. It resists mildew, aging, sunlight, abrasion, and household solvents. It has the lowest moisture absorption rate of the fibers commonly available. It is possibly your best choice.

Polyester fibers are strong and resist mildew, aging, and abrasion. Exposure to sunlight may cause loss of strength.

Nylon fibers are a synthetic petrochemical product. They are very strong and resist staining mildew, abrasion, and moisture.

Modacrylic fibers are a form of acrylic material. They tend to dry quickly and resist sunlight and mildew.

Acrylic fibers are composed mainly of acrylonitrile. It resists mildew, aging, some chemicals, sunlight, and abrasion.

Courtesy Congoleum Corporation

7-9 Sheet-vinyl floor covering is water resistant, durable, and easy to clean. It is available in many colors and patterns.

RESILIENT FLOOR COVERINGS

Resilient floor coverings are a products for use in bathrooms. They are water-resistant, wear well, and are easily cleaned. They provide a degree of rebounding after being bent or depressed. Typical flooring products such as vinyl and rubber can be a bit slippery when wet, but a rubber-backed throw rugs and bath mats provide good footing.

Vinyl floor coverings are available in sheets and individual tiles. The tiles are easier to lay but will often let moisture into the subfloor if the cracks between them open as the subfloor ages.

Vinyl sheet flooring is a polyvinyl chloride product that has a top layer of vinyl and a composition backing (7-9 and 7-10). Vinyl composition floor tiles are composed of vinyl resins, pigments, plasticizers, stabilizers, and fibers. Both products are available in a wide range of patterns and colors.

Sheet-vinyl composition floor covering is available in rolls 9 and 12 feet wide and up to 50 feet long. Thickness can vary from 0.69 to 0.224 inches, so check this before you buy it.

Vinyl composition floor tiles are available in 9-, 12-, 18-, and 36-inch squares and some rectangular shapes, typically ⅛ and ³⁄₃₂ inch thick.

7-10 This vinyl composition sheet flooring sets the tone for the bathroom with the walls a lighter tan and the white fixtures and wainscot prominently displayed.

Courtesy Congoleum Corporation

Vinyl flooring is bonded to the subfloor with the adhesive that is recommended by the flooring manufacturer. The adhesive is troweled on and the vinyl is laid over it, smoothed, and rolled with a heavy metal roller.

It is important that the subfloor be perfectly flat and smooth. If it is damaged, either repair the damage, fill all holes, and cracks, and drive in all nails sticking up, or better still, cover the old subfloor with a plywood, hardboard, or oriented-strandboard underlayment. Again be certain no nail heads are above the surface and fill the cracks between the panels with crack filler. Any irregularities will eventually show through the resilient flooring.

SOLID-WOOD FLOORING

Solid-wood flooring is a durable, attractive flooring covering material. In bathrooms it can be used effectively in areas away from moisture, as the toilet area and along the bathtub. It is nice in a dressing area. Wherever used in a bathroom it should be sealed and finished with coatings providing a high degree of resistance to moisture. Urethane and acrylic coatings are often used. A painted wood floor is shown earlier in **7-2**.

In Chapter 5 see **5-14** for a bath with wide plank solid-wood floors. In Chapter 3 see **3-19** for a wide plank wood floor with a natural finish.

Solid-wood flooring can be installed using unfinished strips and then sanded and finished after installation. If you plan to do the job yourself, consider using factory-finished flooring.

The most commonly used flooring is strip flooring, typically available in 1½-, 2-, 2¼-, and 3¼-inch widths. It has a tongue on one side and a groove on the other (**7-11**) and is generally ⅜ ½, and 25/32 inch thick. It is available in a number of hard- and softwoods including Southern pine, oak, maple, beech, and pecan.

Tongue-and-groove strip flooring is installed by blind nailing through the tongue into the subfloor as shown in **7-12**. Usually a nailing machine is used. This prevents damaging the edge of the flooring. If you use a hammer, drive the nail close to the flooring and finish setting it with a nail set. This is slow but will work (**7-13**).

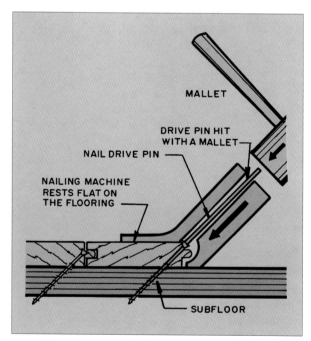

7-12 The best way to nail tongue-and-groove solid-wood strip flooring is with a nailing machine designed especially for this job.

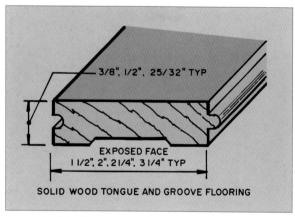

7-11 A typical tongue-and-groove solid-wood strip flooring.

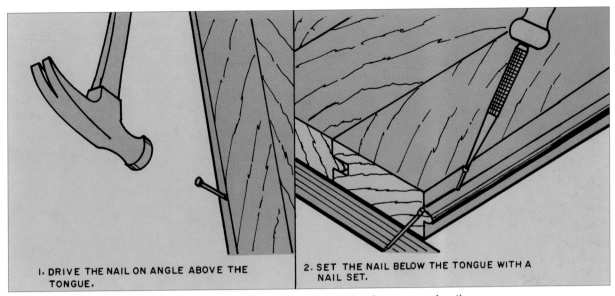

1. DRIVE THE NAIL ON ANGLE ABOVE THE TONGUE.

2. SET THE NAIL BELOW THE TONGUE WITH A NAIL SET.

7-13 You can install tongue-and-groove solid-wood flooring with a hammer and nail set.

Prefinished wood flooring can be nailed to the wood subfloor as described for unfinished wood flooring. Some manufacturers recommend that you lay a 6-mil polyethylene film vapor barrier over the subfloor.

Wood flooring is also available in square parquet blocks. It is available in solid-wood or laminated-wood blocks (7-14).

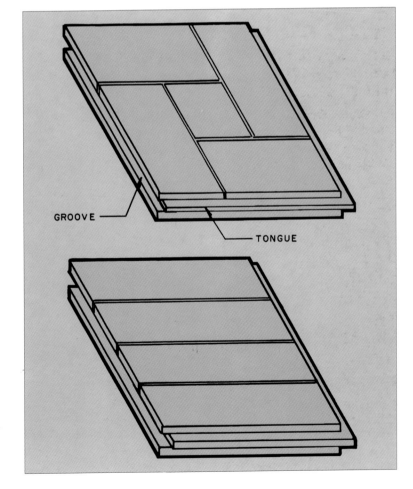

GROOVE

TONGUE

7-14 Wood parquet flooring is available in laminated and solid-wood blocks.

LAMINATE FLOORING

Laminate flooring consists of a high-pressure plastic laminate outer surface over a medium-density fiberboard core (7-15). It is available in planks 7¼ inches wide and four feet long and in 15½-inch square tiles (7-15). The plastic laminate is much like that used on countertops but is many times more durable. It is recommended that it not be used in areas with high temperatures, high humidity, or large quantities of water. It would be an excellent flooring material for bathroom areas not exposed to water such as a dressing area.

Laminate flooring can be laid over existing flooring, such as wood, vinyl, and ceramic tile. It is a floating floor in that it is not nailed or glued to the subfloor or old finished floor; these are covered with a foam padding and the laminate pieces are laid over it (7-16). The pieces have tongue-and-grooved edges glued together forming one large sheet of flooring. They rest (or float) on the foam pad below.

WALL & CEILING COVERINGS

The choice of wall and ceiling finish materials is an important part of setting the overall appearance of the bathroom. As mentioned in the floor discussion hard glossy materials, such as ceramic tile, give a completely different atmosphere from warm wood paneling. In addition some materi-

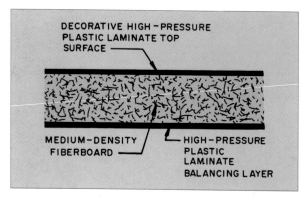

7-15 Laminated wood floor covering is made by covering a medium-density fiberboard core with a high-pressure plastic laminate on top and a balancing layer on the bottom.

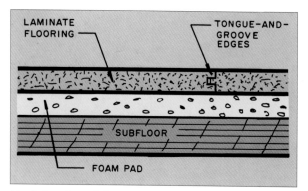

7-16 Laminated floor covering is laid over the subfloor or the existing flooring. It floats on a special foam pad.

7-17 The warm, durable floor tile were placed on the wall, forming a wainscot. The wall above was painted.

als are more expensive and require skilled labor to install. The most commonly used wall finish materials are ceramic tile, wood paneling, wallpaper, and paint over gypsum drywall. Ceilings are usually painted or papered. Whatever you chose, remember it must be able to resist high humidity and be cleaned.

CERAMIC WALL TILE

Ceramic wall tile is a popular bathroom wall covering. Typically it is laid about four feet up the wall and the surface from there to the ceiling is either painted or covered with a washable vinyl wall covering (commonly referred to as wallpaper). Ceramic wall tile is hard, moisture resistant, and easy to keep clean. A water-resistant grout is worked into the spaces between the tiles. Use a grout recommended by your tile dealer for this purpose.

In 7-17 is an interesting application of ceramic tile on a wall. The floor tile are used on the wall forming a wainscoting, and the wall is painted above it. Another interesting installation is in 7-18. Here the bathtub and custom-built shower walls and wainscot are covered with a white ceramic tile trimmed with a brown trim tile that matches the aluminum and glass shower surround. The shower floor and bathroom floor are also ceramic tile. The floor tile is used to finish the walls above the wainscot to the ceiling.

7-18 The shower and tub walls as well as the other bathroom walls are all finished with ceramic tile. Notice the tile trim color matches the shower enclosure framing.

Courtesy Alumax Shower Enclosures

Ceramic wall tile is an excellent wall covering wherever water is likely to get on the wall. In 7-19 it covers the wall above and below a pedestal lavatory. The edge is finished with a bullnose tile. The surrounding wall can be finished with vinyl wall covering or be painted. This is less expensive than tiling the entire wall, yet provides critical protection.

Probably the walls around the lavatory get the greatest exposure to water. The lavatory shown in 7-20 has no protection and the vinyl, coated wall covering will eventually spot and stain. Water will also leak between the countertop and the wall, causing damage to the drywall below. A satisfactory solution is shown in 7-21. The backsplash keeps the water from running

7-19 Small areas of ceramic wall tile can be installed wherever protection from moisture is required.

down the wall, and the ceramic tile provides a water-resistant, easily cleaned wall surface.

To prepare a wall for ceramic tile use cement backer board in any area where it will be subject to water, such as in a shower or at a lavatory. If the lavatory top has a water-resistant backsplash you do not need cement backer board. For the rest of the walls you can bond the tile to gypsum wallboard. It is recommended that you use a mortar that is not damaged by water. It costs more but will be worth it in the long run.

7-20 The wall covering around this lavatory will eventually spot and stain and need to be replaced.

7-21 This installation using a backsplash and ceramic tile gives satisfactory protection to the wall.

Wall tiles are available in a great many designs and several sizes, including 4¼-, 6-, and 8-inch squares and a 4¼-inch octagon. Various trim tiles are used to finish the edge of the tiled area. Trim tiles are also laid within the field of wall tiles to provide a decorative horizontal or vertical feature (7-**22** and 7-**23**). Bullnose tile are used to finish the edge that does not butt a wall, floor, or ceiling. If you have a ceramic tile floor and want a sanitary base along the wall, install a cove base. If the wall is not to be tiled select a base with a bullnose edge. If you will tile the wall use a square edge tile (7-**24**). You can form a square corner by not using a base.

Courtesy American Olean Tile Company

7-22 Ceramic tile covers the bathtub platform and serves as a wainscot. A striking decorative ceramic trim is used to accent both.

7-23 This rounded decorative ceramic tile trim provides a finished edge and horizontal emphasis above the ceramic tile lavatory countertop.

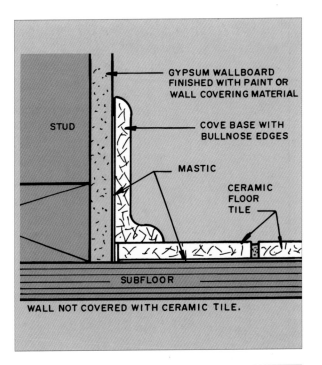

GYPSUM WALLBOARD FINISHED WITH PAINT OR WALL COVERING MATERIAL

COVE BASE WITH BULLNOSE EDGES

MASTIC

CERAMIC FLOOR TILE

STUD

SUBFLOOR

WALL NOT COVERED WITH CERAMIC TILE.

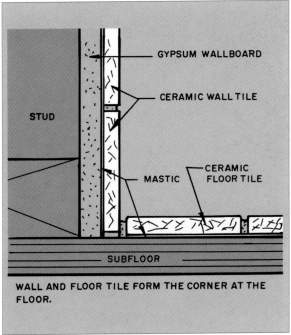

GYPSUM WALLBOARD

CERAMIC WALL TILE

CERAMIC FLOOR TILE

STUD

MASTIC

SUBFLOOR

WALL AND FLOOR TILE FORM THE CORNER AT THE FLOOR.

7-24 (Left and above) Various special tiles are available to finish a wall installation.

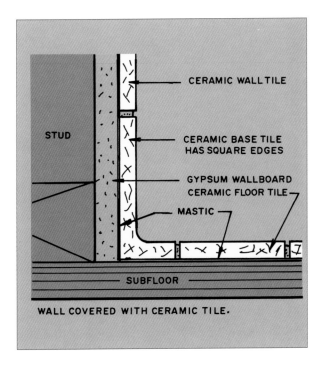

CERAMIC WALL TILE

CERAMIC BASE TILE HAS SQUARE EDGES

GYPSUM WALLBOARD
CERAMIC FLOOR TILE

MASTIC

STUD

SUBFLOOR

WALL COVERED WITH CERAMIC TILE.

WOOD PANELING

Wood paneling can add a feeling of warmth to the bathroom and can be stained to the wood tone you like (7-25). However be certain the finish coats are durable and can resist damage from the high humidity in the bathroom. A durable finish coating will also provide a surface that can be easily cleaned. Avoid the use of wood paneling where it is possible it could occasionally become wet.

Paneling could be solid wood or a plywood panel with a wood veneer on the outer surface or a hardboard or particleboard panel with an overlay that has a printed wood image.

Solid-wood paneling is typically ¾ inch thick (actual) and 5½, 7¼, and 9¼ inches (actual) wide (7-26). It is available as flat boards, as shown in 7-27, or with various machined edges with tongue-and-groove joints, as shown in 7-28. Cypress, cedar, and redwood have little expansion due to heat and moisture, and high resistance to decay and attack by fungus.

Courtesy Kohler Company

7-25 The warm wood walls and dark pedestal lavatory combine to form a restful, attractive atmosphere.

Courtesy Alumax Bath Enclosures

7-26 This solid-wood paneling has been installed on a 45-degree angle, referred to as a herringbone pattern.

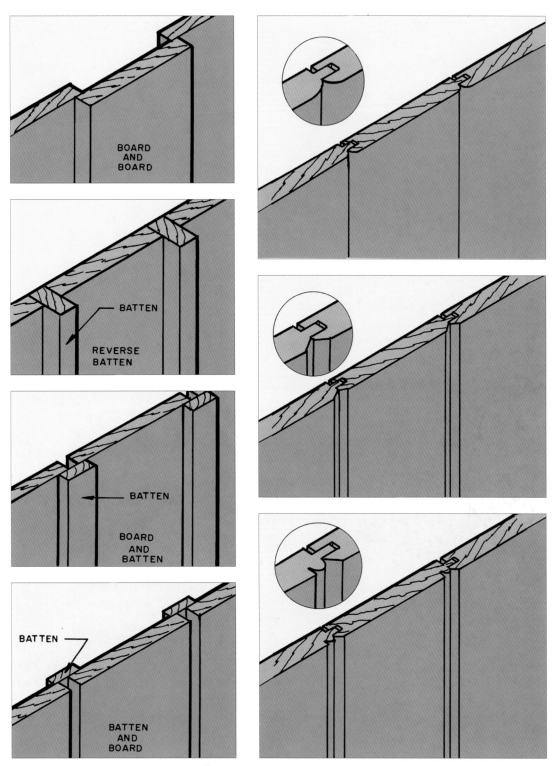

BOARD AND BOARD

BATTEN

REVERSE BATTEN

BATTEN

BOARD AND BATTEN

BATTEN

BATTEN AND BOARD

7-27 Square-edge solid-wood paneling can be installed using battens.

7-28 Solid-wood paneling is available with tongue-and-groove joints.

Solid-wood paneling can be installed vertically (**7-29**), horizontally (**7-30**), or in a herringbone pattern as shown earlier in **7-26**. When installing paneling vertically, you will need to place blocking between the studs (**7-31**) on new construction or place 1 × 3 inch nailers on the old gypsum wallboard if you are remodeling (**7-32**). Horizontal solid-wood siding can be nailed directly to the studs if it is ⅜ inch thick or thicker.

Courtesy Merillat Industries

7-29 This bathroom lavatory cabinet is blended in with vertically applied solid-wood paneling from the wainscot.

Courtesy Merillat Industries

7-30 This natural-wood lavatory is complemented by the horizontal solid-wood wall paneling.

CONSTRUCTING BATHROOMS

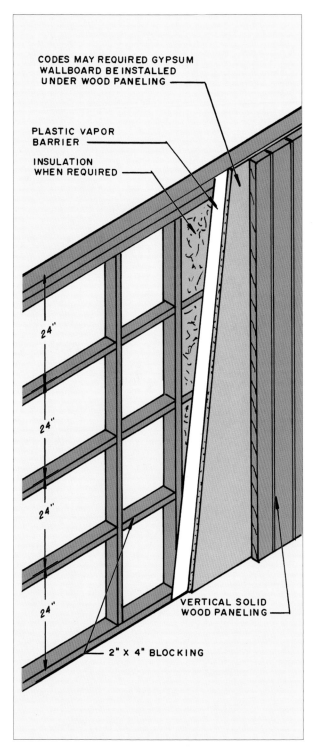

CODES MAY REQUIRED GYPSUM WALLBOARD BE INSTALLED UNDER WOOD PANELING

PLASTIC VAPOR BARRIER

INSULATION WHEN REQUIRED

24"

24"

24"

24"

VERTICAL SOLID WOOD PANELING

2" X 4" BLOCKING

7-31 Vertically applied solid wood paneling requires that horizontal blocking be installed between the studs.

GYPSUM WALLBOARD

16" OC

1" X 3" NAILERS

SOLID WOOD OR SHEET PANELING

7-32 When installing vertical solid-wood or sheet paneling over an old finish wall, install horizontal nailing strips.

Plywood, hardboard, and **particleboard panels** are available in ⅜-, 5/32-, 3/16-, and ¼-inch thickness and in 4 × 8 foot sheets. These large panels have the advantage of being more stable than solid wood and present fewer joints. Joints are where the moisture is going to penetrate the wall so the fewer the better. The panels typically have V-groove joints and several V-grooves machined 16 inches O.C. so they appear as a series of individual boards (**7-33**).

Install sheet paneling to 1 × 3 inch nailers spaced 16 inches O.C. as shown in **7-32**. You can also glue plywood and hardboard paneling to a sound gypsum wallboard partition (**7-34**). Drive a few nails into the studs to help hold it as the adhesive sets. Building codes require ½-inch gypsum wallboard behind it as a firestop. If you care to install sheet paneling horizontally, it can be nailed to the studs if it is at least ⅜ inch thick. Again, a gypsum drywall firestop is required.

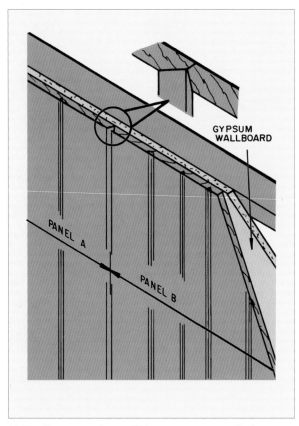

7-33 Sheet paneling will have some type of edge joint and often V-grooves cut on 16 inches O.C. to simulate solid-wood paneling. You can nail through these grooves.

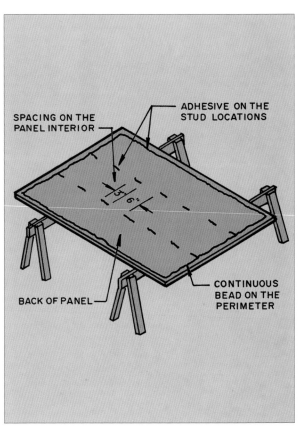

7-34 Sheet paneling can be glued to sound gypsum wallboard.

7-35 The gold shower enclosure and white lavatory are enhanced by the light-colored wall covering. The green and pink design sets the color pattern for accessories.

WALL COVERING (WALLPAPER)

Wall coverings is a term used to describe the product commonly referred to as wallpaper. The available products go beyond rolls of paper with printed designs. A common product has a paper base but has a vinyl finished surface giving it a moisture-resistant property. It can also be lightly washed to remove daily soils. It is widely used on bathroom walls and ceilings (7-35).

Wall coverings come in rolls and have decorative borders also available in rolls (7-36). The range in colors and patterns is great and these can provide the final and major feature of your bathroom (7-37). Select colors that are coordinated with the colors of the tile, floors, fixtures, and accessories (7-38). The ceiling will most likely be a different pattern and be light in color and have little obvious decoration.

Before installing the wall covering you will nees to prime the gypsum drywall. Use the primer recommended by your wall covering dealer. If there is old wall covering on the wall and it is sound, you may apply the new over it.

However, most prefer to use a stripper solution and remove the old paper. If you are covering a painted wall you will have to lightly sand the paint with a fine abrasive paper to dull the surface. This is needed to make the wall covering adhesive bond to the wall.

You can buy wall covering materials that have an adhesive already on the back. You wet the strip in a special pan and place it on the wall. Those wall coverings not prepasted require you apply the adhesive on the back before setting it in place on the wall. Prepasted coverings do not seem to bond to the wall as tightly as those using wall covering paste.

7-36 The distinctive vinyl-covered wall covering border frames the bathtub and is coordinated with the light-patterned wall covering. It would be a good idea to put ceramic tile on the wall from the tub platform to the bottom of the decorative border.

7-37 This vinyl-coated wall covering provides a bright sparkle to the bathroom and enhances the molded-marble lavatory and gold faucet. Notice the wall outlet is also covered so it blends into the pattern.

7-38 This Joan Miró lithograph and a bath towel are coordinated with the colors in the wall covering.

7-39 These white cabinets backed up with light-painted walls will make the bathroom seem larger.

PAINT

Interior wall and ceiling paints are constantly being improved. They are easy to apply and cover well. Cleanup after painting is easy because most use water as the solvent. Generally acrylic or latex paints are chosen. They are available in a high-gloss, a semi-gloss, and flat finishes. The high gloss provides better protection against moisture and mildew. It can be wiped down with a damp cloth. Finishes with satin or flat coatings will eventually be harmed by humidity. The acrylic high gloss would be the best choice, but a semigloss is quite acceptable.

A painted wall is very easily damaged if hit. However, the gypsum drywall damage is easily repaired and the area can be repainted.

When selecting a paint, be sure to consider the colors of the fixtures, floor, and accessories. Remember, a dark color will make the bathroom seem smaller whereas white walls will make it seem larger (7-39). A light color on the ceiling will help reflect light, making the room brighter. In most instances, a bathroom with ceramic tile or vinyl wall covering materials will have the ceiling painted.

CONSTRUCTING BATHROOMS

Additional Information

The National Kitchen & Bath Association is a professional organization representing over 7,000 industry professionals across the U.S. and Canada, including manufacturers, dealers, designers, products, etc. Related publications are available from:

National Kitchen & Bath Association
687 Willow Grove St.
Hackettstown, NJ 07840-9988
800-843-6522, www.nkba.org.

Specifications for making buildings accessible by the physically handicapped are in the report *ANSI-A117.1*, produced and available from:

American National Standards Institute, Inc.
11 West 42nd St., 13th Floor
New York, NY 10036

The *Americans With Disabilities Act*, itself, and *Guidelines* are available from:

U.S. Architectural & Transportation Barriers Compliance Board
1331 F Street N.W., Suite 1000
Washington, DC 20004-1111

Other trade organizations and government agencies that may be helpful include:

National Association of Home Builders
1201 Fifteenth St. NW
Washington, DC 20005

National Sanitation Foundation
P.O. Box 1468
Ann Arbor, MI 48106

Resilient Floor Covering Institute
966 Hungerford Dr., Suite 12B
Rockville, MD 20850

Lighting Research Institute
120 Wall St., 17th Floor
New York, NY 10005

U.S. Environmental Protection Agency
Office of Drinking Water
401 M St. S.W.
Washington, DC 20460

Water Quality Association
P.O. Box 606
Lisle, IL 60532

Selected Bibliography

DeChiara, J., J. Panero, and M. Zelnick. *Time-Saver Standards for Interior Design and Space Planning*. New York: McGraw-Hill, 1984.

——— *Time Saver Standards for Housing and Residential Development*. New York: McGraw-Hill, 1984.

Merritt, F.S., and J.T. Ricketts. *Building Design and Construction Handbook*. New York: McGraw-Hill, 1994.

Spence, W.P. *Carpentry & Building Construction*. New York: Sterling Publishing Co., 1999.

Spence, W.P. *Finish Carpentry*. New York: Sterling Publishing Co., 1995.

Sweet's General Building and Renovation, Catalog File. New York: McGraw-Hill.

Sweet's Group. *Kitchen and Bath Source Book*. New York: McGraw-Hill.

Index

Metric Equivalents

[to the nearest mm, 0.1cm, or 0.01m]

inches	mm	cm	inches	mm	cm	inches	mm	cm
⅛	3	0.3	13	330	33.0	38	965	96.5
¼	6	0.6	14	356	35.6	39	991	99.1
⅜	10	1.0	15	381	38.1	40	1016	101.6
½	13	1.3	16	406	40.6	41	1041	104.1
⅝	16	1.6	17	432	43.2	42	1067	106.7
¾	19	1.9	18	457	45.7	43	1092	109.2
⅞	22	2.2	19	483	48.3	44	1118	111.8
1	25	2.5	20	508	50.8	45	1143	114.3
1¼	32	3.2	21	533	53.3	46	1168	116.8
1½	38	3.8	22	559	55.9	47	1194	119.4
1¾	44	4.4	23	584	58.4	48	1219	121.9
2	51	5.1	24	610	61.0	49	1245	124.5
2½	64	6.4	25	635	63.5	50	1270	127.0
3	76	7.6	26	660	66.0			
3½	89	8.9	27	686	68.6			
4	102	10.2	28	711	71.1			

inches	feet	m
12	1	0.31
24	2	0.61
36	3	0.91
48	4	1.22
60	5	1.52
72	6	1.83
84	7	2.13
96	8	2.44
108	9	2.74

inches	mm	cm	inches	mm	cm
4½	114	11.4	29	737	73.7
5	127	12.7	30	762	76.2
6	152	15.2	31	787	78.7
7	178	17.8	32	813	81.3
8	203	20.3	33	838	83.8
9	229	22.9	34	864	86.4
10	254	25.4	35	889	88.9
11	279	27.9	36	914	91.4
12	305	30.5	37	940	94.0

Conversion Factors

1 mm	=	0.039 inch	1 inch	=	25.4 mm	mm	=	millimeter
1 m	=	3.28 feet	1 foot	=	304.8 mm	cm	=	centimeter
1 m^2	=	10.8 square feet	1 square foot	=	0.09 m^2	m	=	meter
						m^2	=	square meter